The Reality of Partnership
Developing education business relationships

Editors: Bob Gibbs, Roy Hedge, Elizabeth Clough

Longman

THE REALITY OF PARTNERSHIP: DEVELOPING
EDUCATION BUSINESS RELATIONSHIPS

Published by Longman Industry and Public Service Management,
Longman Group UK Ltd, Westgate House, The High, Harlow,
Essex CM20 1YR, UK.
Telephone: (0279) 442601
Fax: (0279) 444501

First published 1991

A catalogue record for this book is available from the British
Library

ISBN 0-582-08487-3

Printed and bound in Great Britain by
Biddles Ltd, Guildford and King's Lynn

Contents

Acknowledgements   v

Foreword: Richard Field OBE, Chairman J & J Dyson
           PLC, Chairman Sheffield TEC   vii

Preface: Bob Gibbs, Elizabeth Clough and
           Roy Hedge   ix

Glossary   xiii

Section I   Partnership: Principles and Purposes   1
Chapter 1   Partnership Principles   3
            John Woolhouse
Chapter 2   Partnerships for sustained economic success   24
            Ivan R. Yates
Chapter 3   Managing partnerships: taking the people
            into account   46
            Bob Gibbs, Roy Hedge and Elizabeth Clough

Section II Partnership in action   63
Chapter 4   Partnership issues in the UK   65
            Sean Lawlor and Andrew Miller
Chapter 5   Partnership and the flight from fancy: the
            promotion of partnership policy in HE   83
            Harry Gray
Chapter 6   Partnership 16–19: possibilities and pitfalls   93
            Michael Austin
Chapter 7   Partnership: one school's experience   105
            Graham Elliott

iv Contents

Chapter 8   Partnership in a development project:
            The Teacher Placement Service   115
            Bill Fisher and Peter Davies

Section III Partnership developments: some
            possible futures   131
Chapter 9   A new role for partnerships   133
            John Krachai
Chapter 10 Assertion of the north — partnership
            for regional development   146
            Michael Harrison
Chapter 11 Towards total quality in education   162
            Bill Walton

Endpiece: Emerging themes and issues: 176
            Elizabeth Clough, Bob Gibbs and Roy Hedge

Notes on contributors   179

Acknowledgements

Editing a book of this kind is itself a partnership activity and we are indebted to many personal and professional friends and colleagues, especially in Sheffield, who have helped us in our practice, thinking and writings.

We are extremely grateful to the contributors for the stimulating discussions which we had with them in the formative stages of this book and for their willingness to meet tight deadlines in delivering manuscripts.

In addition we would like to thank Peter Revill, ex-Compact Director in Rotherham, for his challenging and helpful reading of early drafts; the chief executives and senior officers of various TECs and LECs, members of the Partnership Support Unit of the Employment Department, members of the Centre for the Study of Comprehensive Schools (UK) and staff at the Centre for Education and Industry at Warwick University for their informative and supportive comments; staff and members of the European Conference Board (Brussels), members of the National Association of Partnerships in Education (Virginia, USA), Tom Donahoe of the Pacific Telesis Foundation (California, USA) and Barbara Barnes of Managing Excellence in Education (California, USA) for their insights and global perspectives; members of the British Rail Civil Engineers (York), especially Brian Davis, Hugh Fenwick, John Lowe, Nick Beilby, Sean Heslop and Nigel Ross, for building partnerships of real value and quality.

We would like to thank Roger Henwood at Longman's for his enduring patience and encouragement and, finally, particular

vi   Acknowledgements

thanks to Sandra Quince for managing the production of this
book in draft form with consistent good humour, great skill and
professionalism.

Bob Gibbs
Roy Hedge
Elizabeth Clough
May 1991

Foreword

Imagine a community which is thriving with activity, exciting and fun to be part of, where business prospers and employees and organisations work together to develop the full potential of each individual. There is equal opportunity for all to learn throughout life by upgrading their skills and knowledge through a qualifications structure, thus enhancing their standard of living.

This community has a strategic plan which has the flexibility to respond to exciting new initiatives. The plan is driven forward by the community and is regularly monitored, analysed, renegotiated and improved by the people. The plan reflects the community strengths, needs and aspirations. It is clearly understood and its progress is communicated throughout the community to establish strong feelings of ownership, active involvement and high levels of empowerment to influence the plan for the better.

Is this a complete fantasy? Or can it be realised through partnership? What is certain is that quality strategic planning, democratically approached within the community can only come about if the public and private sectors (including social, community and voluntary services) work together in genuinely collaborative ways. Partnership cannot be a one way activity; in successful partnerships there is learning on all sides. I know from experience that the work involved is continuous and hard, and that among the many successes there will be failures where the integrity of the partners will be severely tested. Partnership is no soft option for education or business.

Training and Enterprise Councils throughout England and Wales and Local Enterprise Companies in Scotland can act as co-ordinating bodies for all quality training and enterprise in local and regional communities. TECs and LECs are themselves new partnerships and, as such, need to earn their credibility in the whole community. To be successful and effective organisations, serving all sectors of the community equally, they will need to gain the confidence of all partners involved. These are formidable tasks.

In TECs we need to continue to learn what partnership means, and what it means throughout organisations, from the top to the bottom, if we are to achieve the goals we have set ourselves. The mission statement of the Sheffield TEC is *to improve the economic prosperity and quality of life for all in Sheffield through a Training and Enterprise Partnership and investment in people*. In other words, it relies crucially on the notion of partnership.

This volume explores the principles, purpose and practices of partnership. It reminds us that there is a history of education and business working together which we would do well to study and learn from — we are not, after all, starting with a blank sheet of paper. If we are to nurture the spirit of partnership, so essential for building strong, healthy and vital economies and communities, it will require vision, flair, energy and commitment from everyone engaged in the enterprise.

The variety of perspectives, the range of ideas and the approaches to partnerships which are embodied in this book make it important reading for all who are concerned with creating and sustaining quality partnerships which will contribute to the education of young people, to the re-establishment of a vibrant economy and to the creation of capable and confident communities to take us into the next century.

In a nutshell, partnerships will be successful where there is real teamwork, a clear sense of direction, regular effective meetings of the team and, perhaps most importantly, staying power. Don't just talk about partnership — go for it!

Richard D. Field, OBE
Group Chairman, J & J Dyson PLC
Chairman, Sheffield TEC

Preface

Partnerships between the education and business communities in the UK are in a state of rapid growth and development. There is widespread support for promoting partnership activity and the UK government is actively stimulating this by providing financial support and encouraging the setting up of organisations to realise the potential advantages of partnerships. Whilst the origins of contemporary partnerships lie in the USA, the last decade has seen the evolution of partnerships in a European context which show significant differences from the US experience.

This book comes about as a result of our collective work and experience over recent years in contributing to partnership development in various forms. Over this period we found ourselves repeatedly posing the question 'What and who are partnerships for?' Our conviction then and now is that partnerships have much to offer local communities, regions and the nation as a whole, but that, all too often, they fail to match the high expectations placed on them. Partnerships have been created with great urgency yet there appears to be a relatively weak conceptual base on which to develop a coherent rationale and to establish common understanding for the present and future development of partnerships. Some activities taking place under the partnership banner fall considerably short of the ideal of mutual collaborative learning and have failed to make explicit the connections between the social, economic and political contributions to the quality of life in communities.

This collection of writings is intended to stimulate and extend the debate around the notions of partnership which will lead to action that is informed, intelligent, enduring and based on quality relationships. The broad aims of the book are to explore the current interpretations of education business partnerships, to critically appraise some examples of partnership in action, to propose new models and strategies for developing the concept of partnership, and to develop principles and practical guidelines to inform those involved in partnerships.

Since the late 1980s, the pace and scale of the partnership movement in the UK has been considerable and has taken various forms, for example the setting up of a Partnership Support Unit at the Employment Department, the inauguration of locally based Education Business Partnerships, Compacts, DTI Teacher and Headteacher Placement Schemes. These initiatives, taken together with those curricular and staff development innovations in schools, colleges and higher education establishments with a clear brief to foster and encourage positive relationships between education and business (e.g. SCIP, 'Project Trident' TVEI, National Curriculum and Enterprise in Higher Education programmes), constitute a powerful imperative for the traditionally separate worlds of business and education to find out what they can learn from each other. The Training and Enterprise Councils and Local Enterprise Companies have a crucial and demanding role of overseeing these connections, enabling and facilitating new relationships and evaluating the quality and effectiveness of developments.

We anticipate that the audience for this book will come from all sectors of the education business partnership movement. It is intended for individuals from education, business, government, the research community and for groups specifically assigned to co-ordinate and support partnership development. Our expectation is that it will complement existing literature by providing an historical perspective, management strategies, critically appraised exemplars of practice and emerging issues for the future.

In order to give the book overall coherence we have separated the chapters into three broad sections. Section I focuses on partnership principles and developments. Section II explores partnerships in action and, finally, section III develops possible future partnership agendas and scenarios.

The opening chapter by John Woolhouse traces the genealogy of partnerships, develops a taxonomy of partnership activity and highlights some of the fundamental principles which should underpin partnerships. This is followed by a contribution from Ivan Yates who, through an economic analysis, forcefully argues the need for radical action particularly by government to revitalise and regenerate the wealth creating sectors of the economy. Section I ends with a chapter by the editors which addresses some of the management issues and problems that partnerships create and offers some complementary ways of managing partnerships to go beyond the technical and functional. Section II covers a spectrum of partnership action. Sean Lawlor and Andrew Miller continue the story of partnership development and raise issues which emerged from their research into a number of Compacts around the country. Partnerships in the context of higher education are taken up by Harry Gray who leads us into an argument that partnerships, in a more sophisticated form, need to become integrated into the curricula of higher education. Michael Austin develops the 16–19 view of partnerships and using exemplars of good practice, raises fundamental issues concerning the reform of 16–19 education. One secondary school's experience of partnership is featured in the chapter by Graham Elliott. The final chapter in section II is authored by Peter Davies and Bill Fisher who write about one of the more recent arrivals on the partnership scene, the Teacher Placement Service.

Service III is about some possible futures for partnerships and John Krachai begins by suggesting a controversial new role for partnerships. Michael Harrison writes provocatively in terms of regional partnership development taking as his example the north of England. The final chapter is written by Bill Walton in which he discusses what education can gain from high quality partnerships. The endpiece, written by the editors, draws together some of the main themes emerging from this book.

Inevitably, as with any collection of this kind, there are important areas of partnership which are not written about at length. The SCIP initiative, which has made a very significant contribution to partnerships and has been reported extensively elsewhere, is not the subject of a separate chapter but its influence infuses the book as a whole. We are also aware that primary partnerships have only a passing reference and that there is much to be learnt from some of the excellent work in this sector.

Finally, the views expressed in the book are personal to the editors and authors and not necessarily representative of their employing institutions.

Partnership Consultancy
Brockwood Park
Sheffield S13 7QH
Tel: (0742) 691710

Bob Gibbs
Elizabeth Clough
Roy Hedge
May 1991

Glossary of abbreviations and acronyms

AOT   Adult Other than Teacher
BIC   Business in the Community
BTEC   Business and Technical Education Council
CBI   Confederation of British Industry
COMPACT Inner City Partnership with specific focus on urban needs
DES   Department of Education and Science
DTI   Department of Trade and Industry
EBP   Education Business Partnership
ED   Employment Department
EHE   Enterprise in Higher Education
ERA   Education Reform Act
ET   Employment Training
FE   Further Education
FEBP   Foundation for Education Business Partnership
FHE   Further and Higher Education
GCSE   General Certificate of Secondary Education
GDP   Gross Domestic Product
GEST   Grants for Educational Support and Training
HE   Higher Education
INSET   In-Service Education and Training for Teachers
LEA   Local Education Authority
LEC   Local Enterprise Companies (Scotland only)
MESP   Mini Enterprise in Schools Project
NAPE   National Association of Partners in Education (USA)
NVQ   National Vocational Qualification

R&D	Research and Development
ROA/RAE	Record of Achievement/Record of Achievement and Experience
SATRO	Science and Technology Regional Organisation
SCIP	School Curriculum Industry Partnership
SEO	Society of Education Officers
SILO	School Industry Liaison Officer
TEC	Training and Enterprise Councils (England and Wales)
TEED/DE	Training Enterprise and Education Directorate of Department of Employment
TPS	Teacher Placement Service
TVEI	Technical and Vocational Education Initiative
UBI	Understanding British Industry
WISE	Women into Science and Engineering
YT	Youth Training

Section I

Chapter 1: Partnership principles

John Woolhouse

Prologue

The 1980s brought a wave of reform and innovation unprecedented in the history of the British educational system.[1] This decade and the early part of the 1990s has been marked by a surge of interest and enthusiasm for new forms of collaboration between education and business that has spread across the United States[2] and Canada, Australia and New Zealand, and many parts of Europe[3,4] including the UK.[5]

What social, economic and educational pressures are driving this epidemic of education-industry partnerships and 'compacts'? Why are the 'partners' investing time and effort in such ventures, and what are their purposes in so doing? Who are the 'partners', and what forms and structures do partnerships take? What activities and programmes are they undertaking? How do they develop, and how are they organised, managed and resourced? How many will survive for a sufficient period of time to fulfil the purposes for which they were formed? How is the contribution of any given partnership to be evaluated, and will the results justify the time and effort invested?

The task of finding any coherent answers to these questions is complicated by the diversity of purposes, constituents, activities and sponsoring agencies which are a feature of the 'partnership movement', particularly in the USA.[6] The US Department of Education reports that 140,800 'partnerships' had been established by 1988; in the UK hundreds of private and government sponsored partnerships, and thousands of primary and secondary schools, colleges, polytechnics and universities are engaged in collaborative programmes with business and industry.

The task is further complicated by one characteristic which partnerships share with the businesses and the educational institutions which sponsor them. They are 'dynamic' and 'adaptive' systems. They are constantly changing in response to turbulent external conditions and as a result of the changing perspectives of their members and 'clients'. The 'life cycle' and 'life expectancy' of partnerships are, at this stage in their evolution, difficult to predict.

The purpose of this chapter is to offer a framework within which the nature and function of partnerships can be explored.

The framework (or those parts of the framework that can usefully be summarised within a single chapter) has four dimensions:

- Historical and political contexts
- Issues, agendas and motives
- Structure
- Scope and function.

Each dimension is introduced briefly as a starting point which may help policy makers, practitioners and observers to reflect on some of the questions and issues to which this book is directed.

Writers and researchers who have begun the study of education-industry collaboration in the UK[7] have tended to take as their starting point the 'Great Debate' allegedly launched by Prime Minister James Callaghan in 1976, although in fact the debate had already been joined in the 1960s.[8] They have pointed to the influence of initiatives such as the Schools Council Industry Project in the same period; to the introduction of the Technical and Vocational Education Initiative in 1983; to 'Industry Year' 1986; to the Department of Trade and Industry's 'Enterprise and Education Initiative' in 1988; and to the Department of Employment's more recent action to generate inner-city compacts, and to promote a nation-wide network of partnerships in each of 82 areas of England and Wales in which Training and Enterprise Councils have been established. These and other initiatives and, perhaps most importantly, the local 'forums' and partnerships set up by companies; by schools, colleges and education authorities; by business and professional associations and by partnership agencies too numerous to mention, are a central part of the story.[9,10,11]

But the key to a fuller understanding of the partnership movement lies much further back in our history.

Historical and political contexts

The further back you look, the further forward you can see.

Winston Churchill

The social historian G.M.Trevelyan, writing about education in fourteenth century England, sets the scene:

There was already considerable provision for the education of clerks in reading, writing and Latin. Three or four hundred grammar schools, most of them indeed very small establishments, were scattered through the length of England. They were usually under the control of monasteries or cathedrals, hospitals, guilds or chantries ... but no attempt was made to teach reading and writing to the mass of the people until the eighteenth century brought the Charity Schools.

The two ancient Universities of England already existed ... but until the growth of the college system brought improvement in the fifteenth century the mediaeval student was riotous, lawless and licentious. He was miserably poor: he often learnt very little for want of books and tutoring, and left without taking a degree...[12]

The founders of our education system were private institutions and individuals. In the nineteenth century the founding of Owen's college and Josiah Mason's College laid the foundations for the modern universities of Manchester and Birmingham.

It was with the greatest reluctance that many of the leaders of Victorian society accepted that the government had any role in education. The first government grant on any scale was made in 1833, when the government gave a grant of £20,000 towards the cost of school buildings to the National Society and the British and Foreign Schools Society.

In 1834 the Lord Chancellor, Henry Brougham, gave evidence to the Committee on the State of Education. Asked his views on whether public utility or expediency made it desirable to create a national system of education, he replied:

I do not well perceive how such a system can be established, without placing in the hands of the government, that is of Ministers of the day, the means of dictating opinions and principles to the people... .

The Committee, interestingly in the context of modern debate, fell to discussing the possibility of a *combination of public and private effort*.

Brougham's opinion on the application of government funds was that 'moderate sums' of public money might be used 'to defray this first cost of establishing a school' but not to meet current expenses because a great advantage would be lost:

> But supposing the expense provided for, I am clearly of the opinion
> that one great means of promoting education would be lost, namely,
> the interest taken by the patrons of schools supported by voluntary
> contributions... .

Brougham had already attempted to get parish schools set up at
the expense of industry by promoting in 1816 an enquiry into
the 'Education of the Lower Orders in the Metropolis and
Beyond'. The name of the committee is clearly a product of its
time![1]

The debate went on. it was not until 1870 that the foundations
of a public system of elementary education were laid by
W.E.Forster's Elementary Education Act, and only then to fill
up gaps 'sparing the public money where it can be done without, procuring as much as we can the assistance of parents, and
welcoming as much as we rightly can the co-operation and aid
of those benevolent men who desire to assist their neighbours'.

Twenty years later in 1890, technical education was supported
for the first time by diverting the proceeds of a whisky tax to enable counties and boroughs to provide 'technical and manual
instruction'.

The long and protracted process of building an adequate system of general and vocational education in Britain from the 1830s
to the 1940s has been described by one historian as 'Education for
Industrial Decline'. Barnett's chapter of that title concludes with
the words of the Schools Enquiry of 1868:

> Our deficiency is not merely a deficiency in technical education, but
> in general intelligence, and unless we remedy this want we shall
> gradually but surely find that our undeniable superiority in wealth
> and perhaps in energy will not save us from decline... .[13]

By studying history of education we are better able to see contemporary issues in perspective, and to identify certain trends
which are clearly discernible over a longer timescale. Firstly, that
only in the last hundred years has government emerged as the
principal provider of general and technical education; secondly,
that until the present century private, non-government initiatives have been the driving force for innovation in education;
thirdly, that the roles of private institutions and of government
are in a constant state of flux, each interacting with the other in
different ways at different times. Fourthly, that private institutions continue in many countries to co-exist with 'maintained'
schools and universities. The co-existence of public and private
institutions is demonstrated by the independent schools in
Britain, and by the private universities and colleges in Japan, in
the USA, and in other countries; and fifthly, that pressures on

government to contain public expenditure, and to reduce the burden of taxation may result in serious under-resourcing of public services including education.

P. H. Coombs, in a world-wide assessment of recent trends and changes in education, originally prepared for the International Institute of Educational Planning, argues that there is 'an emerging crisis in world education'. He points to the tension between the rapid growth of learning needs in both the developed and the developing world, to the rise in real educational costs per student, and to the tendency in many countries since the peak levels of 1975 *to reduce* expenditure on education as a percentage of gross national product.[14]

The interaction between public and private funding of education is as crucial today as it was in the early nineteenth century; the world has changed, but the dilemma remains. The way in which it is addressed in our own times will have a profound effect on the role of the 'stakeholders' in every section of the community.

In the UK, the introduction of student loans; government expectations that colleges and institutions of higher education will generate an increasing proportion of their income from fee-earning activities, grants and donations,[15] efforts to ensure that employers bear a substantial proportion of the costs of post-school education and training; and the cool response of the majority of firms to recent efforts to persuade them to provide a significant proportion of the foundation costs of a nationwide network of City Technology Colleges, are examples of this process at work.

The boundaries between government and business responsibilities for the costs of vocational education and training are being pushed backwards and forwards as successive governments agonise on how best to spread the financial burden. In the years that followed the decline of the apprenticeship system in the UK in the 1960s and 1970s, an attempt to redistribute costs was made through the levy-grant system operated by 20 or more Industrial Training Boards set up under the Industrial Training Act of 1964. Weakened by the 1973 Industrial Training Act, all but one of the boards was abolished within 20 years. The Manpower Services Commission, established in 1973, was to take on the role of a 'national training authority', and in the early 1980s to develop the Youth Training Scheme, and other initiatives. Within 20 years the Commission had been replaced, after various transformations, by a division of the Employment Department.

In 1989 a further shift of power of fundamental importance to the partnership movement took place. Eighty-two Training and Enterprise Councils, with two-thirds of their membership drawn from the business community, were established to develop training and enterprise in areas which span the whole of England and Wales, and to administer a total annual budget of £3 billion mainly allocated to Youth Training, Employment Training and to the Enterprise Allowance Scheme and other grants.[16] In Scotland 22 Local Enterprise Councils will perform a similar function.

The announcement by the Employment Department that Training and Enterprise Councils would be offered funding to establish education business partnerships in each area, marks a new and important phase in the history of partnerships in Britain.[17] From an historical viewpoint, the wheel has turned another circle. Government is now entering into contracts with local agencies to promote partnerships in local communities; the Department of Trade and Industry has already funded a major national initiative in support of teacher secondments and of work experience in industry; the Department is now providing funds, to be matched by employer contributions, to support teachers in primary and in secondary schools in developing the theme of economic and industrial understanding in the National Curriculum now being introduced in England and Wales.

The European Community is seeking to promote collaboration in research and development through COMETT,[18] the European Community Programme on co-operation between universities and industry, and through the PETRA programme on 'the vocational training of young people and their preparation for adult and working life'.[19] The European Network of Training Initiatives will seek to emphasise the importance of partnership at a European level, and 'at national, regional and local level to mobilise the collective resources of the public, private and voluntary sectors so as to develop a co-operative or integrated approach to vocational education, training and counselling for young people, and to promote a climate for effective partnership between the agencies concerned'. One of the three main action programmes is designed to create a 'network of training initiatives to be twinned or linked to produce transnational co-operative partnerships'.

Issues, agendas and motives

The first problem, then, is how can we cover the country with good schools. (W.E.Forster, 1870, introducing the Elementary Education Bill.)

The second problem, one might add, is how can we cover the country with enough good businesses to sustain our economy! Schools and businesses are sub-systems within a society which is itself a complex 'socio-technical' and cultural system.[20] The issues with which partnerships are concerned are complex; the motives of the partners are mixed, and are not necessarily either consistent or compatible; agendas are of an infinite variety, and may or may not constitute an effective means of conciliating the problems that they address.[21,2,22] Partnerships are in essence a search for synergy based on mutual understanding; synergy is the achievement of that additional benefit which accrues to a number of systems when they coalesce to form a larger system, or to use a time-honoured phrase, 'that the whole may be greater than the parts'. As the authors of the Dictionary of Modern Thought observe:

In practice, synergy may turn out to be negative, because the totality is ill-conceived or ineffectively organized.

This 'health warning' might well be displayed in the offices of all partnership organisations!

The main issues can be grouped under five headings:

1. Economic issues centering on the challenge of survival in competitive markets and in a global economy.[23]
2. Social issues in the pursuit of social justice, the self-actualisation of individuals, of equality of opportunity and of opportunities for social or 'upward' mobility.[24]
3. Educational issues related to the quality of learning and teaching and to the development and resourcing of accessible, efficient and responsive learning systems.[25]
4. Scientific and technological issues including the advancement of learning, for example through collaborative research and the diffusion of knowledge and know-how, and the exploitation of technology.
5. Labour market and demographic issues, particularly supply and demand for highly qualified 'professional staff', as skill levels continue to rise in many sectors of industry, and in the public services.

A study by the Mckinsey consulting group in 1986 predicted that by the end of this century 70% of all jobs in Europe would require a professional qualification, and that 35% of all jobs would require a qualification at graduate level. More recent studies by the Institute for Employment Research at the University of Warwick suggest that, in the UK, the Mckinsey forecast may even underestimate the rate of change.

The issues thus presented may seem dauntingly complicated. Their complexity should serve as a warning to those who seek quick or facile solutions to the more deep-seated and complex problems. The agenda of partnerships must be wide enough to accommodate both long-term and short-term goals. There are many practical objectives that can be and are being accomplished within a simple framework and within relatively short time-scales. The implication for government departments, for Training and Enterprise Councils and for local partnership agencies is not that they should procrastinate when there is work to be done, but that they should be capable of distinguishing the one category of objectives from the other.[26]

Issues for partnership in the UK are not dissimilar to those often presented in the USA, although there is as yet no movement in the UK comparable to the American volunteer movement which has mobilised a force of three million volunteers from industry and the professions to work with American students, and in particular with disadvantaged students and potential high school 'drop-outs'.

The Business Roundtable, representing the chief executive officers of 200 of the largest corporations in the USA, identifies three reasons why business has become so involved with schools:

i)   Economic survival
ii)   The need for an educated electorate
iii) The moral imperative that says that the people we count on as the workers and the electorate of the future are increasingly those that our education system has not served well.

Business leaders in America have realized that their economic future is inextricably linked to the quality of education provided to their future workforce and they are doing something about it. Partnership is one vehicle of action![27]

Structure

With a name like yours, you might be any shape, almost.
                                                    Lewis Carroll

The term 'partnership' is used in many different ways. In legal parlance a partnership is 'an association of two or more persons for the carrying on of a business, of which they share the expenses, profit or loss'; the term is also used to describe 'the persons so associated collectively'. In less formal usage, a partner is 'one who is associated in any function, act, or course of actions'; an associate, colleague or accomplice, or a player 'on the same side as another'.[28] To understand education business partnerships it is helpful to know when such a partnership can be said to exist. What are the essential characteristics of partnerships? Are there ways in which partnerships can be systematically described, classified, and better understood? Is there any logical way of distinguishing a partnership from the host of 'links' that occur through the normal interactions of education and business, and of informal contacts between teachers and their colleagues in industry and in other professions?

The Employment Department's guide to managing education business partnerships opens with the question, 'What is an education business partnership?' and offers the following definition:

An education business partnership aims to develop a productive relationship between education and business and to convert activity into results. It may be defined as a joint venture between educators and employers in a local community to raise the aspirations and achievements of individual learners, to allow them to maximise their potential and to enable them to become part of a skilled and adapt able workforce. Its distinctive feature is a formal agreement committing the partners to work together to improve education and employment opportunities in their local area.[29]

Definitions of this type, however carefully constructed, do not of themselves provide an adequate basis for understanding the nature of partnerships. The first, which is discussed in this section, is *structure*, and the second which is discussed in the following section, relates to the *scope and functions* of partnerships, and to the *habitats* in which they exist. Structure, is the equivalent of the 'ground plan' in biology, and is discernible by observation. Five divisions are used in this analysis, although many more divisions and sub-divisions might be added. The five are:

(1) membership
(2) relationships
(3) undertakings and guarantees
(4) constitution and legal status
(5) sources of funding.

The term 'school' is used for simplicity throughout this section, but each combination may consist of a college, polytechnic, university, business school, research institution or other educational body. The word 'firm' may also apply to a public service,[30] professional or voluntary organisation as well as to as to industry and commerce.

12   The Reality of Partnership

1. Membership

Almost any combination of members and categories of membership are possible. Both numbers and categories are likely to change during the 'life-cycle' of the partnership. The most commonly found arrangements are:

- *Pairing or twinning*

  This is the simplest form of partnership and is made up of a single firm and a single school.

- *Single institution with multiple business partners*

  Many schools have built up a 'portfolio' of partnerships with firms which enable them to collaborate with businesses of different size and character, to draw on expertise in different professional, technical or scientific fields, and to work with different sectors of industry.

- *Single firm with multiple educational partners*

  A number of large UK firms, for example BP and the Rover Group, have established partnerships with networks of schools, usually but not necessarily situated in the 'travel to work' areas of major company sites. Comparable arrangements can be found in firms which have established a network with university or polytechnic departments or with business schools. A variation on this theme arises when a single agency or association, for example the Banking Information Service or the Engineering Council, sets up collaborative arrangements with a network of educational institutions.

- *Multiple partnerships*

  Partnerships involving substantial numbers of schools and firms have been established through the work of Chambers of Commerce, Education Industry Forums, Local Employer Networks and other agencies, in many communities in the UK. The number of multiple partnerships is currently being extended as Training and Enterprise Councils proceed to establish new partnerships, or networks of partnerships.

2. Relationships

Some partnerships are independent, free standing, and without formal affiliation to any other partnership. They may prefer independence to affiliation.

However, in many towns, cities and counties 'networks' of partnerships are being established in particular areas or localities. Community-based local partnerships operate within a network of regional, county-wide or city-wide partnerships linked, and possibly co-ordinated, by a mega-partnership, which may be an independent regional forum, or which may involve one or more Training and Enterprise Councils, education authorities and leading employer, trade union or community organisations.

The 'mega-partnership' already exists in some US cities where hundreds of firms are engaged in city-wide partnerships, and in a different form is likely to become more common in Britain as 100 area partnerships across the country are established and funded by the Employment Department through Training and Enterprise Councils or Local Enterprise Councils.

Partnership networks, however, are not necessarily based only on place. Networks may connect partnerships operating within different phases of education, for example between primary and secondary education, between secondary and further and higher education, or all four. Networks may also connect partnerships established by different agencies and those pursuing different themes. The extent to which such networks will promote or hinder the achievement of the aims of the partnerships involved remains to be seen. Much will depend on whether the new networks are managed in a style which supports rather than stifles the growth of local initiatives.

3. Undertakings and guarantees

Partnerships differ widely in the extent to which students in schools and colleges, teachers, and staff in participating organisations enter into agreements or undertakings which define their role and responsibilities within the partnership.

In many partnerships there are no explicit agreements involving students and teachers. One interesting exception is the Rover Group Education Partnership in which a 'partnership contract' is signed by each school, a 'teacher placement planning document' is available for teachers, and a 'learning agreement' is signed by pupils undertaking work experience. A number of other companies and local education authorities have developed systematic procedures intended both to set standards of quality and to meet legal and safety requirements.

The making of explicit agreements between students and employers is, however, at the heart of one of the most recent and distinctive forms of partnership — the 'compact'. Compacts, including school, college, and higher education compacts, are based on agreements under which firms, colleges or institutions of higher education offer guarantees of training, entry or employment to individuals who achieve explicitly stated performance standards. Compacts, therefore, constitute a whole division or class within the taxonomy of partnerships. Variations on this theme can be seen in both British and American schemes in which bursaries or grants are made to individual students who graduate from 'high school', or who achieve entry to specified college courses. Both compacts and grant-awarding schemes are distinguishable from other types of partnership in that they offer direct and tangible rewards to individuals who meet specified conditions.

4. Constitution and legal status

In the preceding paragraph, the use of formal agreements *within* a partnership has been outlined. But what of the constitution and legal status of the partnership itself? What of:

- partnerships in which there is an agreement committing the partners to work together, but in which the partnership has no formal constitution. Many local partnerships operate in this way.

- partnerships which have both agreements and a constitution.

- partnerships which have agreements, a constitution *and* corporate status, for example by the formation of a legal partnership or of a registered company. The Headteachers into Industry Scheme, and a number of partnership agencies, have formed companies limited by guarantee, and it is likely that partnerships set up by Training and Enterprise Councils will use this model. Companies limited by guarantee may also apply for registration as a charity.

Contractual obligations may also arise from the funding arrangements of government or private sponsors.

All education authorities who receive funding for TVEI pilot or extension schemes enter into a contract with the Employment Department which requires that industry is involved in the development of the 14–18 curriculum. Any authority which does not meet this requirement could be held to be in breach of contract. Other government or privately sponsored initiatives may contain legally enforceable conditions which define how specific funds are used.

5. *Source of funding*

The identify of sponsors and the form and level of sponsorship
is another distinguishing feature of partnerships.
Basic distinctions can for example be made between:

- *Publicly funded partnerships* where all or most of the funding
  is provided by government departments or agencies.

- *Partnerships funded jointly by public and private sources.*
  This group includes 'matched funding' arrangements of the
  kind currently used by the Department of Trade and
  Industry. The principle underlying 'matched funding' is that
  public funds up to a specified limit are made available to the
  partnership only on condition that they are matched, on a
  given ratio, by contributions from industry, from fee-earning
  activities, or other sources.

- *Partnerships funded solely from private or 'non-government'
  sources.* Virtually all US partnerships are in this category; one
  of the most marked differences between the USA and the
  UK at the present time arises from the extent to which the
  UK government is involved in the provision of pump-
  priming funds. This position is likely to change in the future
  when the period of government funding comes to an end,
  and partnerships, including compacts, become mainly or
  wholly dependent on private or charitable donations.

Scope and function

"There's no use trying" Alice said, "one can't believe impossible
things." "I daresay you haven't had much practice" said the Queen.
"When I was your age, I always did it for half an hour a day. Why
sometimes I've believed as many as six impossible things before
breakfast."

Lewis Carroll

The classification of partnership by structure has been discussed
in the previous section. A second step in the process is to examine the scope and function of partnerships.

The potential scope for partnerships spans a wide range of
aims and aspirations. Some will be concerned with a single
objective, for example the development of a 'consortium' MBA
in a business school, in which the course is jointly designed,
taught and assessed by staff from the school and from member
firms of the consortium. Some will have a relatively limited

combination of objectives such as the provision of good quality work experience[31] and teacher secondment. Others will set more ambitious goals and will seek to contribute to the economic and social regeneration of a region or a city; to create a 'high-skill high-value-added economy'; to develop a coherent vocational education and training system;[32] or to raise participation rates in post-school education. Some will be mainly 'unidirectional' in the sense that the explicit intentions are to benefit schools, and the benefits to firms are implicit, or expressed only in the most general terms. Others will seek carefully to achieve clearly defined reciprocal benefits for all the partners involved. BP's recent booklet *Education and business: a vision for the partnership* illustrates this by constructing a 'matrix' of activities and outcomes for both sets of partners.[33]

The scope of partnerships will also vary in the size and character of their 'habitat': the geographical area and its economy; urban and rural areas; population densities; distribution and type of industry; declining or expanding economies; number and size of ethnic groups; age distribution and demographic trends; employment and unemployment; skill reserves and skill shortage; labour turnover; the prevalence of poverty and of disadvantage; public and private provision of education and training; 'drop-out' or participation rates.

The main focus in this section is, however, on the functions of partnerships. A set of some 40 functions and activities has been grouped under seven headings: curriculum development; staff development; student benefits; resourcing; research and dissemination; partnership initiatives; and committee membership. Functions and activities can of course be categorised in many different ways. The diversity of activities is endless, but the following list provides a few examples of the more common activities.

1. *Curriculum development.*[34]

Continuous renewal of the curriculum and improvements in the quality of learning are essential to a modern education service. The professional, scientific and industrial communities have a vital role to play in that process:

- Developing the content of subjects and themes within a curriculum, e.g. science and technology, environmental education, careers education, economic and industrial understanding, personal and social development
- Work-based projects, work simulation,[35] work experience,[31] work shadowing and industrial visits

- Enterprise education
- Examinations and assessment, including records of achievement
- Competitions, prizes and awards
- Provision of learning materials.

2. Staff development

Innovation and improvement in industrial organisations, and the development of the curriculum and of learning systems are integral and essential parts of the process of change. The managers and staff of businesses and of schools have much to learn from each other:

- Initial teacher training[36]
- In-service training for teaching and industrial staff
- Secondment of teachers into industry
- Secondment of staff from industry into education
- Management training and development
- Teacher access to training courses in firms.

3. Student benefits and services

The most important service to students and pupils is the access to effective and coherent learning and developmental experiences, but partnership arrangements can provide other benefits, of which a few examples are given here:

- Traineeships and apprenticeships including 'sandwich' courses
- Sponsorship of students at school, college or university
- Guarantees of training or employment, e.g. compacts
- Tutoring or 'mentoring'
- Careers information and guidance.

4. Resourcing

Opportunities for the mutual or reciprocal use of resources by education and by industry to help to enhance the quality of learning in both communities are legion, but frequently remain unexplored. For example:

- Providing or giving access to physical resources, e.g. workshops or laboratories
- Contributions to capital or operating costs
- Lending or donating equipment and software

- Grants for innovation and piloting of new ideas
- Provision of visiting lecturers, teachers, tutors and expert advisers
- 'Industrialists in residence' in schools.

5. Research and dissemination

Collaborative research and development between businesses or public services and educational institutions is one of the oldest and most widely practised forms of partnership. It differs from most other activities in this classification in the sense that the overt objective is usually the conduct of an agreed research or development programme, and although there may be many incidental benefits to both organisations, such benefits are not in most cases the primary purpose of the partners:

- Joint research or development projects
- Contract research
- Funding of research posts
- Establishment of research institutes
- Funding conferences or seminars
- Funding publications or software.

6. Partnership initiatives and agencies

This sixth classification is of a rather different type and relates to the way in which both education and industry are supporting the many partnership organisations and agencies which operate at national or local levels. A number, for example the Schools Curriculum Industry Partnership, based at the University of Warwick, are financed by a combination of affiliation fees, donations from industry, government grants and from fee-earning sources and publications. For example:

- Grants and donations
- Affiliation fees or subscriptions
- Funding of conference and events
- Staff secondments
- Publicity and promotion
- Provision of expert advice.

7. Committee membership

The seventh and last category in this series, which reflects the contribution of individuals to the work of educational councils, committees and governing bodies, is included because it is an important feature of the interface between education and industry. Like other activities in this list, it can and does flourish independently of any formal partnership agreement, although some partnerships may seek to promote the active engagement of industrialists in educational affairs and vice versa:

- Local, regional or national education committees and examing boards
- Polytechnic and university councils
- School and college governing bodies
- Local partnerships and compacts
- National, regional or local committees of partnership agencies
- Educational representation on company boards, advisory and training committees.

Examples of these and other activities and functions will be described in more detail in the chapters that follow, as will the expectations of business and of education, and the potential of partnerships for developing a coherent system of post-16 education and training. At this point, it is important to note that, whilst there is no limit to the variety of activities in which partnerships are engaged, important questions about the *quality and effectiveness* of many activities remain unanswered and largely unexplored.

Conclusion

In this chapter a way of exploring the structure and function of partnerships has been outlined. Many more questions will arise as partnerships develop, and as the number of partnerships grows.

Three questions in particular are relevant to the theme of this book. They relate to the quality of management, to the place of education business in the community as a whole, and to changing perceptions of the role of individual and corporate citizens.

Quality of management is clearly as important in partnership as in any other venture. The Employment Department's handbook on creating and managing partnerships defines six main stages in the evolution of a partnership:[37]

i)   getting started
ii) taking stock
iii) setting goals

iv) managing the partnership
v)   implementing programmes
vi) quality assurance.

The process is, with the exception of the first stage, a continuing process of planning, implementation, feedback and modification. The skill with which partnerships pursue this process will be a key factor in their survival and success, as will the design, at the earliest possible stage, of a strategy of systematic evaluation. The best professional standards of management in business and in education will be essential if partnerships are to survive changing and sometimes turbulent economic conditions and to achieve the appropriate standards of quality in the programmes that they undertake.

Secondly, each partnership will need to assess and re-assess its relationships with the wider community in which it operates.

In 1977 a Committee of Enquiry produced a report, popularly known as the Taylor Report, under the title *A new partnership for our schools*. The report underlined the character of a school as 'essentially a product of *local* considerations' and argued that the governing body of a school should be so constituted that '*no one interest should be dominant* — it should be an equal partnership of all those with a legitimate concern, local education authority, staff, *parents, where appropriate pupils*, and *the community*. Partnerships, if they are to survive and succeed, need to mobilise the resources of the *whole* community.'

Finally, partnerships will need to be vigilant in maintaining the integrity of their policies and practices.

The current emphasis on the role of one particular sector of the community, the business sector, raises profound moral issues, ranging from the possibility of undue influence on schools, and on the curriculum, to the exploitation of partnership as a means of marketing company products and services. The boundaries are not easy to define; the motives of the partners will always be mixed.

The moral issues for partnership can appropriately be set in the context of the duties and responsibilities of citizenship.[38] Partnership is, in essence, a re-interpretation of the roles of individual and of corporate citizenship with particular emphasis on contribution to the well-being of the community, and to the quality and accessibility of education and life-long learning.

The opportunities for partnership arise not only in local communities, but on a wider setting in promoting international understanding and in contributing to a better understanding of global and environmental issues. The *Observer* newspaper on 10

February 1991 carried a report on the involvement of leading businesses 'in schools, cultural initiatives and community projects'. On this occasion business leaders, in the interest of 'corporate citizenship', meeting in New Delhi to discuss the theme of 'Sustainable Rural Development — the Business Contribution', demonstrated that models of partnership now being forged in the industrial countries of the developed world may prove to have an even greater potential in the developing world.

References

1   Maclure, J S, 1986, *Education Documents; England and Wales 1816 to the present day*, Methuen.
2   Training Agency/Business in the Community, 1989, *Education Business Partnerships: Lessons from America*.
3   IFAPLAN, 1988, *School-Industry Partnership — trends and developments in the European Community*, IFAPLAN, Cologne.
4   Blackledge, R C R and Lawson, S, 1990, *Work Shadowing, exchange and partnerships in Europe 1988–1990*, Training Agency.
5   DES, 1990, *Statistical Bulletin*, 10/90.
6   Evans, A, 1991, *Partnerships in America 1990 — a radical agenda*, Employment Department.
7   Jamieson, I, and Lightfoot, M, 1982, *Schools and Industry*; Methuen Educational (Schools Council Working Paper 73).
8   Warwick, D (Ed), 1989, *Linking Schools and Industry*, Blackwell.
9   Meager, E M, and Wise, M L H, 1990, *Directory of Education Initiatives, School Industry Links and Personnel*, second ed.; Engineering Council.
10 Jamieson, I (Ed), 1985, *Industry in Education: Developments and Case Studies*, Longman for SCDC Publications.
11 Smith, D, 1988, *Partners in Change: principles and practice in education-industry collaboration*, Longman for the SCDC.
12 Trevelyan, G M, 1942, *English Social History*, second ed.; Longmans, Green.
13 Barnett, C, 1986, *The Audit of War*, Macmillan.
14 Coombs, P H , 1985, *The World Crisis in Education*, OUP.
15 Ball, Sir C, and Eggins, H, *Higher Education into the 1990s: new dimensions*, The Society for Research into Higher Education and OUP, pp 69–79.
16 Coffield, F, 1990, From the Decade of the Enterprise Culture to the Decade of the TECs, *British Journal of Education and Work*, 4 (1), pp 59–78.
17 Clwyd County Council, 1991, *TECs and LEAs: A Partnership*

Agenda, (Based on a report prepared by the Centre for Education and Industry, University of Warwick).

18 Commission of the European Communities, 1988, COM-METT II, *European Community Programme on co-operation between universities and industry regarding training in the field of technology*, COMMETT technical Assistance Unit, Brussels.

19 IFAPLAN, 1989, *PETRA: the European Community Action Programme for the Vocational Training of Young People and their Preparation for Adult and Working Life*, IFAPLAN, Brussels.

20 Wiener, M J, 1981, *English Culture and the Decline of the Industrial Spirit 1850–1980*, CUP.

21 Cumming, J, 1988, Employer and Educator Expectations for Youth: Fostering the Need for Greater Collaboration and Development, *British Journal of Education and Work*, 2(2); pp 15–25.

22 Wellington, J J, 1987, Employment Patterns and the Goals of Education, *British Journal of Education and Work*, 1(3); pp 163–177.

23 Worswick, G D N (Ed), 1985; *Education and Economic Performance*, Gower.

24 Halsey, A H, *Change in British Society*, third ed., OUP.

25 Spours, K, and Young, M, 1988, Beyond Vocationalism: a new perspective on the relationship between work and education, *British Journal of Education and Work*, 2(2); pp 5–14.

26 Avon Training and Enterprise Council, 1991, *Vision for the Decade*; Avon TEC Development Ltd.

27 Merenda, D, 1990, *Partnerships in Education: an overview of America's Effort*, unpublished paper available from the Centre for Education and Industry, University of Warwick.

28 *Shorter Oxford English Dictionary*, 1983, third ed. Guild Publishing.

29 King, B, Lea, C, and Moroney, G, 1991, *The Partnership Handbook*, Employment Department.

30 NHS Training Authority, 1990, *Recruitment in the 1990s: The Case for a Health Service/Education Partnership*, (based on a report prepared by Professor J G Woolhouse).

31 Miller, A, and Berkeley, J, 1991, *Towards Quality Work Experience for All: Equal Opportunities and Special Needs*, SCIP/MESP Publications.

32 Woolhouse, J G, 1991, *The Principles of Studentship*; Occasional Paper Number 1, Centre for Education and Industry, University of Warwick.

33 Marsden, C, and Priestland, A, 1989, *Working with Education: a framework of business objectives and activities*, BP.

34 Pring, R, 1987, The Curriculum and the New Vocationalism, *British Journal of Education and Work*, 1(3), pp 133–148.

35 Jamieson, I, Miller, A, and Watts, A G, 1988, *Mirrors of Work: Work Simulations in Schools*, The Falmer Press.

36 Bloomer, G, and Scott, W, Industry-Related Activities in Initial Teacher Education: a survey; *British Journal of Education and Work*; 3(3); pp 63–68.

37 Employment Department, 1990, *The Partnership Primer: An Introduction to the Management of an Education Business Partnership*, ED, in association with IBM UK Ltd, the Foundation for Education Business Partnerships and the Centre for Education and Industry, University of Warwick.

38 Heater, D, 1990, *Citizenship: The Civic Ideal in World History, Politics and Education*, Longman.

Bennett, R J, 1991, *Attaining Quality: the agenda for local business services in the 1990s*; Research Papers, Department of Geography, LSE.

Cumming, J, 1987, Curriculum and the World of Work: Issues and Trends in Australian Schools, *British Journal of Education and Work*; 1(3); pp 179–186.

Heywood, J, 1990, Leadership, Management and Education: Lessons for and from Schooling, *British Journal of Education and Work*; 3(3); pp 17–33.

Jones, J, 1990, *Industry-education policy* resource 'pack', BP Educational Service.

King, B, 1991, *A toolkit for evaluation*, E D.

Maclure, J S; 1988; *Education Reformed: a guide to the 1988 Education Reform Act*, Hodder and Stoughton.

Marsden, C, 1991, *Education and Business: a vision for the partnership*, BP.

Merenda, D, 1988, *The Practical Guide to Creating and Managing Partnerships*, National Association of Partners in Education, USA.

Sultana, R, 1990, Schooling for Work in New Zealand: Reproduction, Contestation and Transformation in three High Schools, *British Journal of Education and Work*, 3(3), pp 35–48.

Woolhouse J G, 1988, Organization Development; in *The Gower Handbook of Management*, second ed., Gower, pp 40–53.

Chapter 2: Partnerships for sustained economic success

Ivan Yates

The UK has persistently failed to recognise the value of education and skills and undervalued the importance of manufacturing. These failures go a long way to explaining why for many decades UK economic performance has been inferior to that of comparable countries. Our Gross Domestic Product (GDP) per head is now less than that of Germany, France, Japan, Italy, all of whom have overtaken us in the last thirty years and we are about to be caught up by Singapore (*see* Chart 1). The effects of history, the Empire, two World Wars and until recently North Sea Oil, have obscured this reality.

Our economy is less stable than others, with a large negative balance of payments and generally larger variations in rates of growth, exchange rate, inflation and bank rate, than our competitors. Over the past two decades large sectors of manufacturing industry have been weakened and some have disappeared. That which remains is far stronger than hitherto but is largely concentrated in two main world class sectors, namely pharmaceuticals and fine chemicals on the one hand and aerospace and certain defence related industries on the other. It is this diminished size of the manufacturing sector which is the main cause for concern and the underlying cause of the adverse balance of trade.

In particular we have failed to recognise the importance of skills in relation to productivity in manufacturing, and our education system has badly neglected the training of 16–19 year olds. Associated with a significantly lower participation rate in higher education we are now faced with a very serious skills shortage throughout most of the working population. This will become painfully clear as we try to climb out of the present deep recession.

Chart 1

Real Growth of Gross
Domestic Product
Per Person: 1950–85

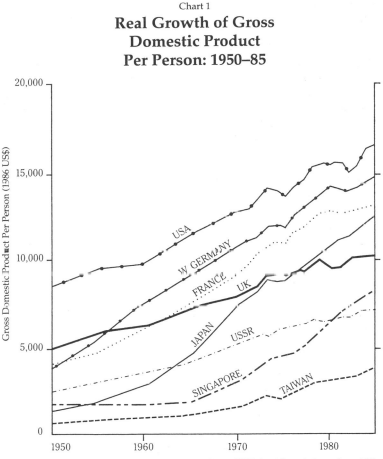

Source : US National Commission on Space 1986

In addition the financial environment for our publicly quoted companies appears to be less favourable than those enjoyed by our competitors, particularly Germany and Japan. The intense demand for steady growth measured by profit, distributed dividends and share price is associated with caution and risk aversion by management. Management reacts by demanding a higher rate of return on investment and research and development (R&D) than is required by the overseas competition. This means that organic growth is restricted and companies are increasingly driven to seek expansion by acquisition. This may achieve short term financial benefits to the shareholder but fails to produce the balanced industrial expansion attained by similar companies overseas. In Germany and Japan, organic growth of companies benefits the whole economy, and thereby on a much wider basis the shareholder in the longer term.

Due to these effects, reinforced by other distortions in the economy, investment in the UK tends to be increasingly concentrated into the non-tradeable sectors, reinforcing the structural distortions. Thus the scope of economic policy options is reduced to a narrow range, involving the reduction of overall growth.

Re-building the manufacturing sector will take time. It will also take significant time to make major improvements in the national education and training system. There are no short-term solutions to the problem of short-termism.

Factors speeding the process should be welcomed. These include inward investment by the Japanese, European and American companies. However there are certain criteria which should be applied. For instance investment should be associated with UK based expenditure on research and development of new products. It is clear that the UK should not be brought into a situation where it is either the supplier of new ideas which are exploited entirely by others, or a screwdriver factory assembling products with the essential know-how and skills residing overseas.

Any solution must treat the sequence of innovation, training and skills and financial investment, as a total system. There are strong interactions and dependencies between all these elements. They all materially effect the overall economy of the country. A co-ordinated approach to the whole problem is therefore essential, forming the right partnerships is one of the keys to success. It also needs significant increases in investment. The objectives will be extremely difficult to achieve and will require a revolution in our national attitudes.

Investment in the manufacturing sector

The situation is serious enough in relation to investment in research, but is particularly so in relation to the development of new products in manufacturing, the level of capital investment and above all, the investment in the training and education of our people — our most valuable resource. Put simply the challenge of a new industrial revolution has to be met. It is a matter of the utmost priority and needs the same focused attention as the

Chart 2
Volume Indices, GDP, Mf, Services
1964 = 100

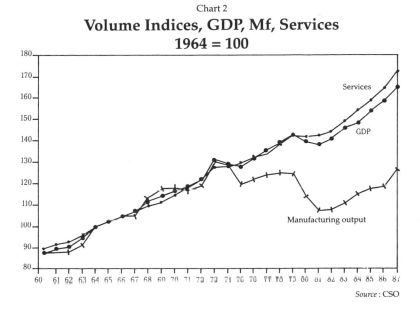

Source : CSO

Government of 1979 gave to setting up the enterprise culture in the UK.

The true situation is somewhat worse than is widely recognised. First, because the actual skills shortage, as Sir John Cassels[1] has said, is even worse than the familiar statistics on skills shortages indicate. Secondly, because most of the predictions for the 1990s are based on the assumption that present trends will continue, that is that the manufacturing industry will recover only moderately and that certain service industries will continue to expand very quickly. These trends have been evident and accelerating over the last decade particularly since the early to mid 1980s (Chart 2).

The UK position in manufacturing is relatively poor in comparison with some of its strongest rivals. Increasing the tradeable sector is the basic way of putting right the balance of payments, and hence stabilising the relationship between inflation, economic growth and exchange rate (Chart 3).

A rough calculation, made for the so called 'Bastille Day' Conference in July 1989,[2] showed that the UK manufacturing sector, (the heart of 'tradeable' activities) has to be increased from about 23% to about 28%–30% of gross domestic product by the end of this century. An increased tradeable sector appears to

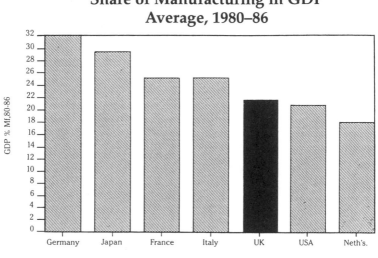

Chart 3

Share of Manufacturing in GDP
Average, 1980–86

Source : OECD

bring other benefits such as lower inflation, better exchange rate and higher growth — very important to the whole economy: as a result there is a 'pay-back' for the investment which brings about this improvement.

Such an increase, to say 28% or 30%, cannot be achieved within a decade by organic growth alone, that is by increasing R&D and by increasing the number of engineering students entering intermediate and higher education. That would simply take far too long and whilst essential, will not of itself achieve significant growth by the end of the decade. The solution therefore involves coupling these national improvements with a policy which welcomes significant inward investment, for instance by the Japanese in electronics and in the automotive industry, in addition to investment by European and American companies. However, inward investment will not provide an automatic or quick solution either. We must also take account of another in-built bias in the UK system, which recently has been against investment in the tradeable sector of the economy. Over the last few years the increase in investment has been heavily in the non-tradeable sectors[3] and this makes it clear that we need to examine the investment mechanisms available for long term projects.

The desired 'target' of growth in manufacturing to 30% was

based on some simple calculations around manpower availability, possible productivity increases and a target of reattaining balance of payments equilibrium. A fairly constant work-force at today's levels and a productivity growth of about $4\frac{1}{2}$ % per year — tough but possible — will satisfy the requirement of equilibrium by the year 2000.

Cambridge Econometrics[4] have put these parameters into their sophisticated model of the economy (Chart 4). This shows a base forecast on the past trends — with chronic balance of payments problems for the next decade. However, if a rise in manufacturing to 30% is simulated, the balance of payments problem is easily resolved by the mid 1990s. But again this is only a simulation. It will not happen 'of itself'.

Chart 4

Returning Manufacturing to 30% GDP
Balance of Payments Scenarios

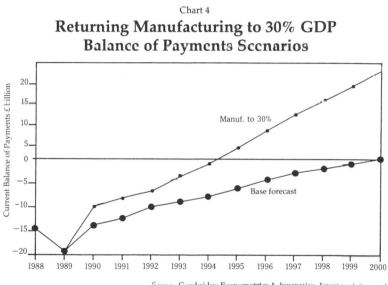

Source . Cambridge Econometrics & Innovation, Investment, Survival

There is a danger that this message will be seen as doom and gloom. It is certainly not intended to be that but there are some very major difficulties confronting the UK; a crisis maybe, but not the sort of crisis which is going to lead to disaster this year, next year or even the year after. It is the sort of crisis which is leading to a steady decline which has to be reversed.

There are some world class centres of excellence in the economy. For instance, the pharmaceutical industries and parts of the chemical industry on the one hand, and aerospace on the other, have been in very good health during the past decade. They also represent two distinct types of industry — those based on chemistry which process large quantities of material in what is a large scale version of the laboratory, and those based on physics where the technologies emerging from the laboratory are used in very different forms. It is the assembly of a range of technologies, integrated by the designer to form a new product, which is the essence of engineering and manufacturing in this sector. For several reasons it is the engineering sector of manufacturing which is weakest; the primary reasons are almost certainly that it depends so much on the skills and knowledge of its workers, and the way that their knowledge is organised, that it is more vulnerable to a shortfall in the national knowledge base, as well as on our attitude to the use of such knowledge in manufacturing. But there are several reasons why, despite this national shortcoming, aerospace has been successful. It has historically been able to attract engineers and skilled craftsmen and women and has been supported in its technological base, and in selling into export markets, at a level comparable with industry in the USA and France. In particular, without support in the form of Launch Aid — long term, repayable, patient money — the UK would simply not be in the Civil Aeroengine and Aircraft business today, and for instance the £13 billion worth of civil aircraft, engines and equipment exported in the last five years would not have been sold.

The UK expends on average (having correctly allowed for defence expenditure),[5] barely 2% of GDP on research and the development of new products. Other developed countries are increasing their expenditure to over 2.5% and in the case of Japan towards 3% as a national objective. But what is equally important is the fact that R&D expenditure tends to increase faster than the growth of an economy which is healthy. The effect of low UK expenditure in R&D has been to suppress growth in manufacturing industries which have continued to suffer decline as a percentage of the total economy. This holds back long-term growth in the economy, as well as producing a poor trade balance.

I have already said that there is a positive correlation between the size of the manufacturing sector and the growth of a national economy, and that what is clearly needed is an increase in the size of the manufacturing sector as well as a steady improvement in its efficiency. I have therefore suggested that in the UK we need, as a national target, to increase the proportion in manufacturing to closely approach 30% of GDP by the year 2000. However, we have to make sure that our industry does not contain too many screwdriver factories and we must ensure, by whatever means we can, that there is an appropriate level of local innovation and development. Wherever possible this should be in partnership with higher education and at the same time we must increase the total expenditure on our national R&D. Compared with the competition the shortfall is significant; to increase R&D expenditure to competitive international levels would cost an extra £1.5 billion in 1991. We have to achieve these targets as soon as possible.

The challenge

Economic strength in the modern world is based on innovation and technology which finds its way into the economy through manufacturing industry. Properly managed and nourished — that is with the right financial and educational environment — this process produces steady growth. The UK at large, and this applies to politicians and to those who advise them, has not come to terms with this whilst our rivals, unfortunately, understand it only too well.

Government in partnership with industry, must come to recognise and fulfil its responsibilities in order to achieve long-term strategic objectives in the wealth creating manufacturing sector of the economy. To do this we have to go beyond the process of setting annual budgets without an overall strategic objective; there is a danger that the annual budgeting process can become almost an end in itself — but in reality it is sustained investment over a long period of time which produces success. Yearly targets might have been appropriate two centuries ago when life was dictated by the annual cycle of seed time and harvest; or even 150 years ago when it took only six months to knock together a wooden battleship. It is quite inappropriate in a modern industrial society with natural development cycles of several years, or for that matter in the educational world where it can take many years to produce significant changes.

Investment in education and training

A rise in the quality of support for manufacturing from education and training is crucial if we are to reach our objective of staying in touch with the leaders in the world's economic race. Investment in manufacturing requires much more than investment in the latest machinery. Wise managers know that there are three primary parameters by which good manufacturing can be recognised:

(i)   investment in R&D — the emphasis is on big D, Design and Development of new products
(ii) investment and innovation in the manufacturing processes and the way they are organised
(iii) investment in training and education for everyone involved.

Unless we get the overall level and balance between all three correct, and tragically in the UK in general there is significant under-investment in all three, we simply cannot get the virtuous cycle of profitability that we need in order to make the investment for the future. We have to break out of the vicious circle of under-investment in all three sectors.

We must then consider people and invest in them and in the development of their attitudes, as the key to success.

Investment in education and training also comes under three headings so far as industrialists are concerned:

1) National education and training as it is delivered to the door — the Chancellor budgeted approximately £23 billion for 1990, which is, of course, a huge public investment.
2) Specific training required at the start of working life.
3) Continuous retraining which goes on throughout working life — today some people are retrained every seven years and in high tech industries such as electronics and aerospace, more frequently.

The recent report, *Training in Britain*[6] estimated that 2) and 3) above together cost employers — including Her Majesty's Government — £14 billion in 1986/87 — this is split into approximately £4 billion for initial training and £10 billion pounds for retraining.

The reason why nearly all British industry is seriously disadvantaged by a relatively poorly educated and trained workforce, and by the problem of recruiting competitive levels of staff, can be seen by comparing the qualifications of school leavers in the UK, France and Germany (Chart 5).[7]

A consequence of this qualification profile can be illustrated by comparing the UK range of the qualifications of those entering the engineering professions in a number of competitor countries (Chart 6). The UK seems competitive at the top levels going into engineering, but falls down badly on graduate numbers, compared to France and Germany, and is particularly deficient at technician and craft levels — activities which are crucial to efficient development and manufacturing.[8]

In the past manufacturing industry has been able to fill some of the gaps in the work-force, in particular the ranks of

Chart 5
Highest Qualification of
School Leavers

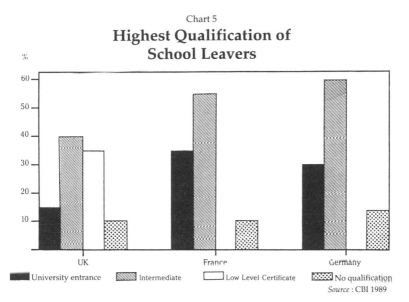

University entrance   Intermediate   Low Level Certificate   No qualification

Source : CBI 1989

Chart 6
Engineering Qualifications

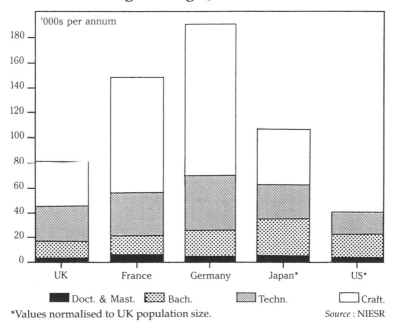

Doct. & Mast.   Bach.   Techn.   Craft.

*Values normalised to UK population size.   Source : NIESR

technicians, by training those with ambition from the flow of high
quality apprentices in its own training schools. But the supply
from this source, has begun to dry up very rapidly. The fall off to
about one third since the 1960s is very serious indeed.

The even greater shortage of technicians than graduates has
several important consequences. With the relatively easier supply of graduates there is the tendency to use them as technicians
— an easy option with bad knock-on effects. This can not only be
de-motivating, but results in weakness in the sector where innovation and efficiency-producing changes have the greatest effect
— that is in the application of developments, rather than in the
research laboratories.

Today we have to look to all levels of the work-force for invention and improvement, a message that is so clearly understood by
the Japanese, and which industry in the UK is beginning to recognise. In manufacturing (indeed, in all businesses) I believe it
should clearly be recognised that it is the responsibility of each
successive level of management to maximise the freedom for
innovation and creative thinking in the people for whom they are
responsible. This responsibility for encouraging creativity, whilst
maintaining an overall discipline within the organisational structure of a company, should be repeated successively through every
level of management, up to the Board and Managing Director of
the individual business, and onwards so that it becomes one of
the key responsibilities of the board of the parent company.

A further key issue, which is frequently neglected, is the
strong relationship between skills and productivity. It is the
increase in productivity — or the reduction in the cost of high
quality manufacturing — which is central to economic success.
Recognition of this relationship is widespread, but it is rare for
the full effect to be recognised. Very large differences in efficiency and cost levels have been identified in the careful research
work of Professor Sig Prais.[8] Put simply, direct comparisons
between similar factories, or for that matter hotels, in the UK and
Germany show dramatic differences due to the higher levels of
skills — and better organisation — in Germany.

UK industry then is faced with a double burden. First it has to
make up the deficit in the training and skills level of new recruits
as delivered from the education system; thus it is immediately at
a disadvantage compared with international competition because
of this additional expense. Second, it has to continuously
upgrade those in work to international levels. Since 80% of the
work force in the year 2000 is already in employment in 1990,
and many at a skill level less than the competition, industry has

a second additional burden. The consequence is reduced efficiency, lower profits and hence less money available for re-investment: a vicious circle of low productivity, low wages and shrinking market share is formed.

Special measures will have to be adopted if we are to break through these difficulties quickly. There is a good case for national support to industry either by direct grants or levies, or by some positive tax rebate system, such as is used to support expenditure on R&D in most developed countries.

When the comparison is focused on the skills level achieved at various ages between the UK, France and Germany, it is probably true to say that of all our educational problems, that associated with the high rate of drop-out between 16–19 years is much the most serious.

A target has to be set for the level of participation in full-time education and training in this critical 16–19 age group. It means a national target such that nobody could be employed unless they are undertaking appropriate vocational training on an organised basis with the aim of achieving internationally recognised qualifications. This target is far tougher even than the second target — namely to double the post-19 participation rate in full time education and training from 15% to about 25%, as the CBI and others propose. I believe that this may well be too modest, and that we should aim for as high as 30% early in the next century.

The target of raising standards for that part of the population aged 16–19 not going on to full-time higher education has to be achieved first, because it underpins the whole system. It also provides the basis for the flow of skilled technicians, and well trained semi-skilled people, which supports the whole of the trained technical population, particularly professional engineers. As we have seen, the shortage of skilled craftsmen and women and of technicians is currently even more acute than the shortage of graduate engineers.

There is a growing belief, which I think is correct, that in order to achieve these objectives for all people up to 19 years old, we will require some form of legal framework. It cannot be left to a simple matter of choice or voluntary participation. If some legal framework can be agreed in order to achieve this objective, then it is a matter for urgent action by government to implement it.

Government has a responsibility for setting out the legislative framework within which industry and education can come together in partnerships at all levels to facilitate the collaborative pursuit of solutions to these problems. Without such activity, we will fail. There is another important factor — particular attitudes to industry, which are characteristic of the British, need to be understood and taken account of in the determination of solutions to the problem.

Attitudes to industry

Difficulties in the British real economy, particularly in manufacture, run parallel with, or may even be caused by negative attitudes to the industrial world and to those values which can promote a successful manufacturing sector.

One definition of genius is the capacity to take infinite pains. Unfortunately the desire of the British is to give out an aura of 'effortless achievement', the preferred 'one-shot' solution, rather than to be thought to be grinding away solidly at a problem.

In the UK there is a curious habit of treating life as some sort of game. A relatively poorly educated work-force, which is one of the primary problems in the UK, is an example of so-called 'non-level playing field' within Europe. But it is only the British who are foolish enough to refer to the fierce competitive world as a playing field. Everybody else knows that it is in reality a battlefield on which will be decided the future prosperity of each nation. The British have not, as a nation, come to understand and accept that this is the criterion by which we are now judged, and the success or otherwise of our efforts is what determines our standing in the world.

Unfortunately success in these areas means dealing with extremely complex problems, which need a lot of thought and meticulous analysis. To many of us this is merely boring. We simply, as a nation, have not given the matter enough thought and attention.

The market signalling device for careers in a free economy is of course the price obtained for the unit of labour, and the prospective price — the career ladder. For graduates, (see Chart 7) the signalling device seems firmly jammed in favour of the less tradeable sectors of the economy. As I have already argued, those signals are being respected by much of the cream of our national talent, and not just by the élite. The effect is seen in most of the work force.

Potential recruits are well aware of this situation which currently disfavours manufacturing and engineering against the rest of the economy. They are also conditioned by media coverage of national economic issues. Negative attitudes

Chart 7

Salary Progress, Graduates
by Sector

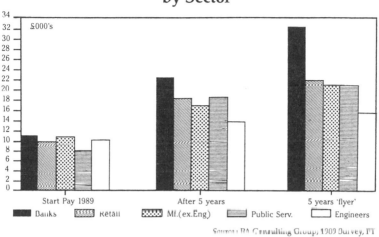

Source: BA Consulting Group, 1989 Survey, FT

Chart 8

Careers Seriously
Considered by Students

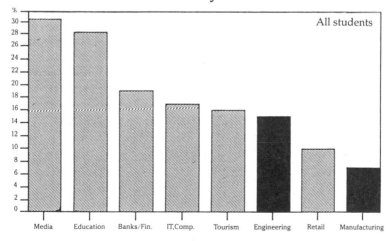

Source : FT, GB Research, 1990

towards manufacture are endemic in British public opinion — the survey of British social attitudes, 1988/89[9] indicated that graduates believe that the manufacturing sector of industry is much less well run than banks, or the civil service, or the City. These unfavorable attitudes feed adversely into the career aspirations of students, as indicated by Chart 8.

Partnership across the world of industry, education and government is urgent if we are to make an impact on negative attitudes to manufacture.

Education and training : some solutions

Education and the economy

To a customer of education, rather than an educationalist, it seems that education and training are essential components in generating 'national competence'. The difference between education and training, academic or vocational knowledge, skills and learning are well rehearsed and a diversion from the central argument in this chapter. I intend to concentrate on analysis of the evidence presented earlier in the chapter and apply it to develop a structure on to which the planks of policy can be fastened.

Whilst education and training can be regarded as having a narrow or personal objective, or a broader social objective, they can equally be regarded as having economic objectives. Unless the economic objectives can be achieved at the national level — and quite clearly in comparison with our competitors we have failed in the UK — then we cannot enjoy the real wealth which can be used to pay for the others.

The skills market and re-training

In the area of vocational training, industry, through the CBI has been very active. I am pleased to have been a member of the task force[7] which drew up a set of recommendations which are widely known. These include a crucial role for government in establishing a coherent vocational, educational and training policy and a significant emphasis on enabling individuals to maximise potential through training.

Various other activities have effectively contributed to the call for action on education and training. Groups like the Fellowship of Engineering, the Institution of Mechanical Engineers and the Employment Institute, to which the Royal Society of Arts has added its voice and efforts, actively support investigation into the key issues surrounding the future industrial and economic health of the UK. There can be no longer any doubt about the direction in which we should be going; we simply have to meet the challenge of a new industrial and educational revolution. Unfortunately we do not have much time.

National objectives for education and training

The main issues for education and training appear to be:

1) The output of the education system post 16 years must be significantly increased by the year 2000, with at least 65% of the population participating to National Vocational Qualification 3 (NVQ3) level and 25% to degree level. The former will require some legislative framework, the latter, possibly, an extension of the use of General Degrees. The cost of these changes will be in the region of £1.5 to £2 billion each year. We cannot take too long to achieve these targets. We should aim for the 16–19 targets by the middle of the 1990s and to reach the target for higher education before the end of the century. These targets are very tough, but the French have made encouraging progress over the last two decades. If the UK can get its act together there is no reason why it should not produce similar improvements.

2) It is essential that government, education and industry accomplish meaningful partnerships to fulfil these aims and that a tangible framework of legislation, grants, assessment and investment priorities be established. This overall framework must be supported by the creation of a positive and relevant 'learning culture' which is user-friendly and accessible to all.

3) These partnerships must respect the individual — nothing will be achievable without individuals being convinced of the importance of these proposals to themselves, their families and the national well-being. No less important is the fact that they will need to contribute through personal investment.

The cost and the payback

We know that the better companies spend between 2% and 3% of their turnover on initial and re-training programmes. Allowing for the lower requirements in medium and low technology industry and for the fact that small companies do much less, if

Chart 9

Expenditure on Training and Education

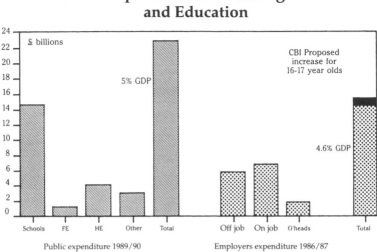

Public expenditure 1989/90   Employers expenditure 1986/87

any, training, then within manufacturing industry the cost is probably in the region of £2 to £3 billion per year. We also know in a general way there is a payoff for such training and education, and for the effective management of the workforce. But I believe that we do not know sufficiently clearly, first, what the payback is for this expenditure and, second, how much greater the payback would be for increased expenditure.

We already spend large sums on education and initial training of young people. Chart 9 shows how the costs are distributed based on the latest information, including the extra cost for the CBI vocational training proposals[7]. There clearly has to be a large increase. It is not good enough to slide gradually up to continental levels of annual input on these vital activities — we have to make good the long backlog of dereliction as quickly as we can if we are to maintain a position as a first rate European nation.

In addition, there is the cost of the massive programming of re-training and updating of the workforce already in employment.

The likely extra costs of these drives are difficult to estimate — but we are talking surely of another several billion pounds per annum. It is very important to establish a good estimate of future costs. The question then arises who should pay?

Can, or should, industry shoulder this burden? Inevitably it will take its share. Profit is the lifeblood of industry but it is important to remember that industrial profit levels in manufacturing in the UK had only just got up to the levels of international competition in the rest of Europe before the present recession. Industry will be hard put to make up all these areas of recovery in education and training. We need to get some honest and agreed 'best estimates' of all these figures out on the table. Fudging, for whatever reasons, is completely indefensible. My own back of the envelope calculation suggests that the extra cost for manufacturing industry is in the range of one to two billion pounds per year.

It is important to have an idea of these extra expenditures within industry for two main reasons. First because nearly all companies need to do more training and would be encouraged to do so through hard evidence from others; and secondly because the smaller companies are frequently not in a position to undertake cost-effective training and all too often rely on poaching from larger companies. Large companies are naturally unwilling to train excessive numbers of recruits, or be generous about updating their existing workforce, if they believe they will lose a large proportion in wastage to other companies. They will only become unconcerned about this when excess training capacity is not a cost burden. This means there has to be some form of tax rebate, or a levy system, and a structure put in place which will allow small companies to participate and fund a fair proportion of the total training.

Investing in the 'knowledge base'

Some significant sums of money have been mentioned, for instance additional expenditure within industry of about £1.5 billion per annum to produce a competitive level of research, technology and product development. Secondly some £2 billion additional annual expenditure in education and training is required to achieve the 65% participation to NVQ3 level and some 25% participation to degree level; this is probably an underestimate, but is the right order of magnitude. In addition we might need as much as £2 billion per year to upskill the industrial workforce to international levels.

This is a total of about £5 to £5.5 billion per year, as an investment in the national 'knowledge base'. In addition, commensurate capital investment in physical assets is required.

The central argument in this chapter — that increased investment in education and training will play a major role in increasing the output of our manufacturing base in UK — is of course predicated on a belief in the connection between economic well-being and investment in people. Consistently, we fail to recognise that expenditure of this type must be seen as an investment for which there is pay-back. Unfortunately all too often this pay-back is not recovered by that part of our society which makes the investment. Whilst society generally accepts that the country has to invest in basic science and in education and some of the infrastructure, policy makers and politicians frequently do not apply these arguments to manufacturing industry.

It is also true that the result of investment in skills by the individual and collectively in groups of individuals is frequently undervalued. For instance, the UK Stock Market rarely makes due allowance — with the exception in general of pharmaceuticals — for the research and development expenditure within a company. Nowhere does there appear to be an allowance made for the benefits of the investment which a company makes in the training and re-skilling of its workforce. This is starkly illustrated when the processes at work during a hostile take-over are examined. Usually virtually no account is taken of the mutual investment made both by the company and the individual who may have worked in the company for many years. A new approach is needed to these intangibles; to the investment made by the company in training its workforce, and to the investment made by the individuals not only in their own education and training, but in their contribution to the well-being of the company. These ideas mean a fundamentally changed set of values for the 1990s and the future.

The way ahead — the role of government in creating partnerships between industry and education

There can be no doubt that in the future partnerships between the education and industrial sectors will be key, but equally nothing will happen without effective government leadership and an appropriate framework of finance and legislation.

The difference between academic and non-academic, between training and education, skills and learning are increasingly becoming blurred and the challenge will be for the education system as a whole to promote a much more substantial, balanced and varied output. There needs to be improved access into the traditional academic system and part-time and continuing education will need to grow as well.

Several pieces of 'mechanics' need to be put into position:

- bridges and ladders to provide a variety of routes into and through the education process allowing and encouraging access to all who seek it — these processes will need to cater for all age groups and be accompanied by a variety of financial support mechanisms
- a modular structure for education and training programmes which may each be taken in a number of different ways, such as full or part-time, assessed or not assessed, distant or traditional delivery
- much improved transferability of modules within a national and, ultimately, a European setting must be a clear aim — it is important that this system of 'universal credits' recognises personal achievements and allows for differences in educational routes
- career training and learning opportunities must be available to all regardless of their age — the idea of a through-life education process must be accepted as re-training on a 7–10 year cycle is becoming crucial (and this time period may well tend to reduce as change processes are accelerated).

But these 'mechanisms' can only bring about the desired change if they are set within an agreed NATIONAL FRAMEWORK FOR PARTNERSHIP which has the following characteristics:

- A national infrastructure which creates a POSITIVE CLIMATE for training and education and also provides individuals with an ability to choose time-off, career breaks, secondments etc. The UK workforce seems much more inflexible than in other countries, sometimes due to employer attitudes, sometimes due to the national infrastructure, for example in accommodation or pensions.
- Government must continue to assist individuals in their right to EDUCATION AND VOCATIONAL TRAINING through support by voucher, tax relief, grants and loans. I think there should now be an exhaustive and detailed examination of all possibilities of means of financial support.
- A stronger emphasis on REGIONAL ORGANISATION for higher education would contribute to the rationalisation and transferability of educational and training qualifications. The portability requirement may be first met through, for example, regional Scottish, Welsh, North-West, North East, Midland etc. groupings. There are economies of scale possible and with larger units organisational problems can be solved. There is also a better prospect of developing the

44   The Reality of Partnership

closer community links which are required to establish the wider social relevance of an education system. The TECs seem the best prospect to date and capable of developing their role.

• The further development of *KEY CENTRES OF EX-CELLENCE* in higher education to strengthen leading-edge post-graduate education in critical and new technologies.

• Overall the quality of education must be overseen through *NATIONALLY CENTRALISED ACCREDITATION PROCESSES* which ideally require the merging of academic, vocational and professional groups. There is an urgent need to have much greater clarity of the range of academic, soft and hard skills as an essential part of the process of modularisation and portability. The setting of such broad 'National Education Standards' presents a major challenge which requires many institutional ramparts to be lowered.

In this scenario for the future I would like to see people feeling that a well earned qualification was worth having and as essential for social well being and progress as a house, a motor car or TV.

Finally although we have seen education and training come close to the top of all the political priorities, it is unlikely that leadership for such radical change will come readily from government in the short-term. We must therefore now see the task as the construction of detailed, well organised and effective policy options, followed by lobbying of government with compelling proposals. The basis for this detailed working out of policy must be one of *PARTNERSHIP BETWEEN EDUCATION AND INDUSTRY*. I would personally like to see the core of the studies leading to proposals for policy prepared by a new partnership between engineers and economists — a link singularly lacking so far.

References

1 Cassels, Sir John, *Britain's Real Skill Shortage and what to do about it*, Policy Studies Institute. *See also* RSA *More Means Different—Widening Access to Higher Education* by Sir Christopher Ball and *Employment and Structural Change in Britain: Trends and Policy Options* by Christine Greenhalgh, Employment Institute.

2 *Innovation, Investment and Survival of the UK Economy*, sponsored by BAe, Fellowship of Engineering, PA Consultants and Institution of Mechanical Engineers, 14 July 1990.*

3   Muellbauer, J, and Murphy, A, *UK Economy 2000 Workshop Paper*, sponsored by BAe and Fellowship of Engineering, January 1990. Later published in *Economic Policy*, October 1990.*

4   Industry and the British Economy to the year 2000, Cambridge Econometrics in *Innovation, Investment and Survival*, Fellowship of Engineering 1990.*

5   Yates I R, *Future Aerospace Projects or Engineering the Future for UK Limited*, Royal Aeronautical Society 76th Wilbur and Orville Wright Memorial Lecture, December 1987. *See also Industrial R & R and Public Policy*, European Industrial Research Management Association Conference Papers, Vol. XXXVII.

6   *Training in Britain, Employers Activities*, HMSO, 1989.

7   *Towards a Skills Revolution*, Report of the Vocational Education and Training Task Force, CBI, 1989.

8   Prais, Professor Sig, *NIESR Review*, February 1989.

9   British Social Attitudes 1988/89.

*   *See also* Employment Institute Conference, 17 July 1990 Yates, I R, *Improving Britain's Industrial Performance*.

Chapter 3: Managing partnerships: taking the people into account

Bob Gibbs, Roy Hedge and Elizabeth Clough

If people want to change their environment they need to change themselves... not someone else. Repeated failures of organisations to solve their problems are partially explained by their failure to understand their own prominence in their own environment. Problems that never get solved never get solved because managers keep tinkering with everything but what they do.[1]

Introduction

If you cast your eye across the education business partnership landscape what do you see? What landmarks and features stand out? What climatic conditions prevail? What kind of activity and endeavour is taking place? Who is engaged on tasks and who stands on the edges? How is the activity happening? Who, if anybody, controls or co-ordinates the activity? What sorts of mental pictures and images are conjured up in your mind as you survey the partnership landscape? Is it a 'battlefield, a jungle, a set of tinker toys or a carnival'?[2] Are you part of the landscape or a voyeur of the scene?

How you answer these questions depends on your place in the partnership firmament, your particular view of partnership and is likely to be a good indicator of the ways you see partnership being managed. Whatever your perspective, be it internal or external, the management of partnerships is a problematic, highly complex and skilled affair. The structural and procedural robustness of partnerships will be severely tested in economic, social and political ways over the coming years.

This chapter will analyse the recent history of the management of partnerships, the contemporary approaches, and will identify the problems and issues that seem to be emerging as partnerships aspire to higher levels of maturity. The latter part of the chapter gives some guidelines for action based upon practice. The central argument is that, because partnerships occupy a unique position in our society, transcending traditional organisational boundaries, they require forms of management which are radically different and distinct from traditional and classical methods if they are to make effective interventions into local communities and wider society. We will explore the dominant management model of partnerships to date and look at the potential of integrating a human relations model into this technical-rational model.

Management context

Before the late 1970s partnership activity went under the banner of industry-education initiatives and was seen by educationalists and industrialists as a somewhat peripheral and discrete activity, with limited curriculum connections. These initiatives did not appear to be a high priority on the agendas of either the captains of industry or the policy makers in education. The management of these activities was seen as a relatively unproblematic affair. In the education domain great changes were afoot as the comprehensivisation of secondary education sought to make a grammar school curriculum available to all.

Gradually, as the 1970s wore on, national politicians became increasingly sceptical that education was adequately preparing young people for a fully productive role in the economy beyond school. The British economy was consistently outperformed by its major rivals and the view that this was substantially the fault of the education system gained strength. The idea is still with us. That the education system must become closer to the world of business and better organise itself to prepare young people for their role as producers has become a 1980s cliche. This notion, stated in numerous and often contradictory ways and accompanying practical imperatives as various as the Technical and Vocational Education Initiative (TVEI) and National Curriculum, is the mainspring of the contemporary drive towards education business partnerships.

It is no accident that education business partnerships now occupy a central position on the political stage of the present

Government. It is not necessary to go back very far into the history of partnership activity to see significant shifts in the balance of power, in the importance placed upon partnership activity and in the expectations that have been placed upon partnerships in terms of solving economic problems. As the 1980s unfolded the Government reinforced the principles and practice of an enterprise culture and a free market economy in all areas of life in the UK. There was radical reform in the education service and critical interventions into schools, colleges and higher education institutions that were to have long term and dramatic effects — some of which are still to be cashed through. Some of the more significant events of that process included the extension of the Schools Curriculum Industry Partnership (SCIP) to most local education authorities (LEAs), the pilot and extension TVEI programmes, Industry Year 1986 and its consequent legacy, the DTI's Enterprise and Education Initiative, inner city compacts, the Education Reform Act including the major features of Local Management of Schools (LMS) and National Curriculum. All this has to be set alongside broader social and economic changes of the decade including soaring unemployment figures, the erosion of the manufacturing base and the rise of the finance and service industries, the quelling of industrial disputes through confrontation and legislation to reduce the power of the trade unions (most classically seen in the 1984–85 Miners Strike), the privatisation and selling off of huge nationalised industries (British Telecom, British Gas, Water and Electricity Boards) and perhaps, most controversially, the ill-fated introduction of the Poll Tax and its subsequent knock-on effects in terms of the local funding and control of the education service. Given this backcloth of profound social and economic change the emergence of education business partnerships should not be seen as mere coincidence.

The watershed of partnership development came about in the late 1980s and early 1990s and was a result of a number of key events. The Training Agency (TA) had become an important means of sidelining Department of Education Science (DES) bureaucracy and inserting radical changes into the worlds of education and training. TVEI, Compacts, Youth Training (YT) and Employment Training (ET) were all examples of the enormous power and influence that the TA was then able to command. It may be that the death knell for the TA tolled when the trade union representatives on the TA executive groups refused to support the introduction of ET, thus temporarily thwarting the plans of the then Prime Minister, Margaret Thatcher. Whatever the reason the TA was replaced in early 1990 by the Training and

Enterprise Councils (TEC) which were conceived in a shotgun marriage between Tory ideology and the desperate need to get employers to help create a modern work force. The Training and Enterprise Councils (TEC) in England and Wales and the Local Enterprise Companies (LEC) in Scotland, populated and largely governed by business chiefs, were established along the lines of the USA Private Industry Councils (PICs) but in a more expansive form. The TECs' brief is to provide local action based on local market needs and their agenda includes training, enterprise, education, compacts and education business partnerships. As the economic crisis deepened the part that education might play in either contributing to that crisis or remedying it were debated in reports from the Confederation of British Industry (CBI), most notably the Cadbury Report.

Simultaneously, groups which had been active in the industry-education field for many years including for example, SCIP, Young Enterprise, and Trident began to reach new levels of maturity and impact. Universities, notably Warwick, and polytechnics began to develop centres for education business studies, to respond to the needs in the field. The USA experience was considered to be instructive and many fact finding missions were flown to the US by British politicians, educationalists, policy makers and business people.[3,4] Education business partnerships would occupy a key position on the political stage. Partnership's time had arrived.

It is hard to detect any coherence in partnership management development before 1990. Different initiatives appeared to operate from a variety of philosophical positions — there was no uniform approach or apparent coherence or co-ordination.

At a national level the common pattern has been to provide pump priming money, usually from the Department of Trade and Industry (DTI) or Employment Department (ED), to create central project teams which in turn forge and support networks around the country. 'Shared' or 'matrix management' models have been common, where the people who control and have the power (i.e. the people with the money) are located in different organisations from those on the ground delivering the partnership products. More recently, groups with overarching responsibility for partnership development have emerged — e.g. Foundation for Education Business Partnerships (FEBP), now defunct, the Industry/Education Association and the Partnership Support Unit of the Employment Department.

At a local level the management of partnerships has had more detectable shape, maybe because at this level partnerships are somewhat more accountable to a defined community.

Typically, the professionals engaged in education business partnerships have been seconded from either industry or education; they have locked into local structures such as chambers of commerce, employer groups, local education authorities or whatever and operated through a management/co-ordinating group with reasonably specific objectives and points of action. The arrival of major education business partnership development through local TECs and LECs challenges the plurality of management approaches. As a result of a review of partnership purposes and priorities a new orthodoxy of partnership management is evolving. There are still weaknesses however; the major ones are lack of funding for partnership initiatives, lack of security of tenure for people working on these agendas, and, most importantly, the fundamental problem of addressing large societal problems (either anti-industrial views or anti-intellectual views) through small scale projects.

On the premise that the problems and issues of the past can inform the future we shall try to identify some of the problems endemic to partnerships of recent years.

Problems and issues associated with managing partnerships — some major features

A fundamental weakness and problem facing partnerships past and present in the UK arises from the fact that there has been little recent habit of partnership between business and education. In the world of business, American ideas of collaborative management taken up, particularly in Japan, have seen little take up in western organisations despite being much lauded by western pundits. Collaboration between banks and the companies in which they invest, buyers and suppliers in the industrial process, management and unions, government and business is not the habitual mode of relationship in the UK. Competition and conflict are more the order of the day, except in times of national crisis.[5,6,7,8,9,10]

The reasons for this decline in collaborative spirit are well documented elsewhere and are not the subject of this essay, but this weakness, which sometimes manifests itself as hostility towards co-operation, is an Achilles heel for the social and economic wealth and health of the UK.

Because the idea of partnerships has only been on the agenda at times of crisis other problems have manifested themselves.

Generally, the rationale for partnerships' activities has been weak. Often the stated purposes have been ambiguous, vague or too idealistic to create either a long-term commitment or any sense of motivation from the various groups involved. There has been a reluctance on the part of educators to face up to the harsh economic realities of which they are a part and industrialists have failed to assert in sophisticated ways what they consider to be appropriate curriculum experiences in preparing for working life in the late 20th century.

Partnership activities to date have been typified by gatherings of high level leaders of the education business world over banquets where the rhetoric, like the wine, has flowed with consummate ease. The real action has been limited to small pockets of activity, often in isolation of other events, with the impressive support of the interested few from industry and motivated professionals from education. The problem here has been to achieve commitment at all levels of organisations, rather than just the top and the bottom, and to go beyond the bun fights, conferences and the warm inner glow that people feel as they wax lyrical about the advantages of partnerships. In other words, the task is to move towards a better fundamental understanding of the purposes of and necessity for partnerships. Growth of the habit of partnership requires increased sensitivity to and awareness of differences and similarities between the cultures of education and business coupled with creative approaches to transactions across the boundary.[11]

It is not uncommon for descriptions of education business partnerships to be couched in terms of two sides coming together in some kind of new symbiotic relationship. This analysis is neither particularly helpful nor does it advance a more mature view of partnership activity. Of course people who work in business and people who work in education occupy different cultural worlds. The norms, attitudes, values, beliefs and behaviours that are practised or subscribed to in education and in business are significantly different, but the emphasis has customarily been on the differences rather than similarities, on separateness as opposed to togetherness. Maybe this is a typical British reaction. The managing director of the local company is a consumer of educational services and products in just the same way that the director of education of the local authority is a consumer of the services and products of local business. What is difficult is to recognise that what appear, at one level, to be insuperable cultural clashes, are differences more imagined than real. If the potential partners share their unconscious assumptions and stereotypical views these misconceptions can possibly be neutralised and more dynamic co-labouring and co-learning can follow. The problem of partnership territories is both paradoxical and never changing. The experience of recent years suggests that within the galaxy of education business partnership groups and organisations, there is, on the one hand, the rhetoric of collaboration and co-operation but on the other hand, a high degree of paranoia in partnership work, focused on survival and power. This has led to some unsavoury activity where there has been much secrecy, competition between so called collaborating groups, political power struggles, a high degree of gamesmanship (occasionally engaged in by women) and a lot of spoiling and blocking activity.[6,12] There are strong hierarchies, largely obscure but definitely felt in the partnership world, and this leads to ongoing conflict and tension between those who are supposed to be on the same side of the fence. These hierarchies or power bases rise and fall and it is particularly sad to see partnership activities at both local and national level founder because of an unwillingness to accept the disciplines of collaboration.

A further problem associated with the crisis management of partnerships is that very often the claims for and expectations of partnership activity go far beyond the real possibilities. Partnerships might be seen as attempts to compensate for deeper seated problems to which there are only partial or very complex and expensive solutions. Partnerships cannot compensate for national or local economic mismanagement, lack of social reform or educational short termism. The real problems facing the two key partners at present are that the professionals in the world of education are suffering from overdirection, innovation overload and low morale and the partners from business are preoccupied with survival of their companies, a deepening recession or the escalation of interest rates. The focus of partnership thus far has either been so broad as to be meaningless or so narrow as to be constraining.

The key question facing partnerships is 'Who sets the partnership agenda?' If it is set centrally at a national level then the important notion of partnership being responsive to local community needs is weakened. The arrival on the scene of the TECs and LECs has sharpened the focus on education business partnerships. This could become a mixed blessing in that whilst the TECs and LECs have revitalised and re-stimulated the debate around partnerships they may come to see themselves or be seen as the gatekeepers of partnership activity, the filter through which established education business organisations and groups either gain access or are excluded. Even the promotional literature published by TECs uses a key shaped logo and adopts slogans referring to 'unlocking potential'. So, 'the key is with TECs'. Under these circumstances partnerships may polarise opinion which may result in indifference among the players. Recent indications are that partnership rationales in TEC and LEC regions are too weak to facilitate the necessary emphasis on satisfying real local needs. There is much re-inventing of primitive wheels. None of this situation is helped by discouragingly low levels of funding.

So the recent entry of the TECs and LECs into the education business arena has potential for both positive and negative outcomes. Collaboration across the multiple realities which exist within the cultures of government, business, education, the civil service and the provider groups, set against the diversity of demands and needs from local communities make partnership a daunting task, not to be undertaken lightly. What is clear, taking an historical perspective of education business partnership development, is that it will not be enough to use outdated and inappropriate forms of enabling, facilitating and managing partnerships. This will only begin to scratch at the problems which TECs have been set up to address. Partnerships are between people not structures. People adopt defensive routines and strategies when threatened or fearful of revealing their lack of knowledge, understanding or competence.[13] The education business partnership initiative may well be subverted as people protect themselves from exposure to the difficulty of managing partnerships in effective ways. Real education business initiatives mean radical personal change and new forms of management.

This catalogue of problems may make depressing reading but represents an attempt to go beyond the celebratory nature of most partnership activity and be realistic about the deeper issues which have to be addressed if partnerships are to contribute towards the forging of thoughtful, vibrant economies and communities.

Managing education-business partnerships effectively

Managing educational business partnerships is a highly complex and demanding activity requiring the highest professional skills, a sound knowledge of management of change theory-in-action, an ability to envision the future whilst dealing with the present and, most importantly, a good deal of common sense coupled, with undying faith in people. The acid test for the effective management of partnerships will have two dimensions, first whether the partnership is fulfilling the expectations of its patrons and clients and, secondly, whether or not the partnership is viewed both internally and externally in positive and constructive ways.

The problems facing the effective management of business-education partnerships at the present are like those inherent in any other regeneration programme. There is the legacy and debris of previous education business activity some of which continues in vibrant forms and some of which limps along.

Partnership — the enabling organisation?

Some interesting features of the ways in which partnerships are beginning to be managed are now becoming clear. In one sense the battle of the partnership giants is over, in that the TECs and LECs have a clear political mandate to pursue the education business partnership agenda in vigorous ways. It seems sensible, therefore, to see the future of partnerships in these terms, though many of the issues would be the same however organised.

In order to attract much needed funding to stimulate partnership activities TECs have been impelled into adopting a new orthodoxy of partnership management which could be limited and limiting. The prevalent management models are based upon classical theories of organising and support the notions of technicality and rationality as levers of change and development. There is a danger that little account is taken of the human, social and economic ecologies which contextualise this management model of partnership. These will differ enormously depending upon location in the UK. This is not to say that the classical model is bad or wrong, it is simply limited, bureaucratic and provides only superficial opportunities for change and development.[14,15,2]

There is an enormous amount of evidence for and about change which extends notions of management to include the human relations element, emphasising the importance of communication and the significance of organisational culture in promoting effectiveness.[16,17] A problem for TECs now is that they are in danger of failing to recognise that much valuable pioneering partnership work has already been accomplished. What is required is to move beyond pioneering through the development of systems and controls which integrate and enable education business activity to take place in meaningful and purposeful ways.

The challenge facing the management of partnerships now, particularly for TECs is how to organise and manage the partnerships most effectively i.e. what kinds of structures, systems, procedures and processes should be organised and maintained and, most crucially, how should the people be managed? At what scale should they operate and for what tasks should they be responsible? In what ways are they likely to change over time? How can organisational theory be integrated into practice to create enabling organisations?[18]

If an organisation supporting education business partnerships is to create a framework which truly enables dynamic activity, rather than to foster controlling and limiting mechanisms then there are certain characteristics which are inescapable. For partnerships to be enabling organisations which characteristics would be prominent? The single most important feature is that the enabling partnership places emphasis on the interface between the partners themselves. The role of senior managers in this partnership is then best described by the single phrase 'How can I help?' in the following contexts:

- in managing the organisation and inter-organisational events by handling the human, physical and financial resources in ways that fulfil strategic goals
- in planning and forecasting what kind of supra-organisation is required for the future, hence which opportunities to take up and where to invest time, energy and money
- in shaping the organisation and setting the climate so that everyone can give of their best and feel that their contribution is recognised and valued
- in monitoring and reviewing the performance of the organisation so that a stream of critical decisions informs the action and when things start to go wrong, as they surely will, they can be rectified.

By working in this way, the managers of partnerships from all sectors will be in a better position:

- to envision the future community needs
- to rekindle and maintain the spirit of partnership
- to be clear about wider community advantages and gains accrued through partnership activity
- to replace the notion of ownership of partnerships with a concept of guardianship

- to maintain a clear set of partnership principles and values which relate to day to day action
- to begin to develop a culture of partnership which affects the behaviours of people in partnerships and develops a concept of service.

Towards an agenda for action

The assumption is that there is a real and valuable role for partnerships as organised through TECs and LECs or other organisations, which needs to be matched by a clear vision of how the process of managing training and enterprise can be achieved in ways which help communities. The impression so far is that there has been a great deal of emphasis on structures, board and sub-group membership, guidelines, territories, budgets, stocktakes and bidding for sums of money. The view that technical, rational and functional models of managing partnerships needs to be supported by person friendly, flexible and adaptive processes is well evidenced in the literature of organisational change and development and is confirmed by the life experience of the participants. If applied, this convergence of theory and action could be the liberating force for partnerships.[19,11,20,21]

Partnerships do not exist as separate context free entities, but in different situations and forms within and between other organisations. It is impossible, therefore, to give a prescription for a series of steps which would provide quick fixes and instant solutions. The challenge to partnership management is to develop approaches that deal with the unique problem of managing the boundaries and transactions between TECs, business and education in the particular organisational forms and configurations they have adopted. Partnerships will challenge and test the internal workings and management styles and systems of their constituent organisations. They will encourage innovation and change whilst the constituent member organisations will strive for stability. There are likely to be personality, group and culture clashes both between and within organisations. It is imperative that partnerships at a local and a regional level develop management models which help to create learning networks and hybrid forms of management based on the evidence of participants' experiences. Whilst there cannot be prescriptions or recipes for developing successful partnerships, the evidence does allow the construction of a set of guidelines for ensuring that partnerships exist in a positive climate.

To begin with partnerships will need to establish a vision,

values and principles statement, define clear purposes, develop strategic plans extending up to a two year planning horizon and identify the core people to manage the partnership[22]. A structural framework needs to be established which allows sufficient flexibility to encourage innovation from a base of stability. The critical factor in making all this happen is best encapsulated by the phrase 'taking the people into account'.

Guidelines for action

1. Develop a *clear rationale* for the education business partnership that becomes both a rhetorical vision and a shared script for participants at all levels. Encourage reflective discussion on actual events, linked with small-step, incremental action planning. Think whole partnership but act in focused ways to create hot spots of activity.
2. Work on developing *supportive communication* across the partnership. Communication climate and organisational culture have a great deal in common. The partnership culture will be based upon organisation members' shared perceptions of the partnership reality. Supportive communication climates include elements of description, problem orientation, spontaneity, empathy, equality and provisionalism.[23]
3. Learn about, respect and use in intelligent ways the *history of partnerships* at local, regional and national levels. As partnership activity gains pace there is an overwhelming mountain of information being generated through stock-takes, audits, market surveys, reviews of action etc. much of which has confused and obfuscated more than it has clarified and prioritised. It is important to remember that one person's cold audit is another person's life experiences which should be extended the appropriate respect and acknowledgement.[18,4]
4. *Upskill members of the partnership* in cross-organisational and institutional groups specifically in the following areas: working in teams, improving communication, strategic planning, project management, creative responses to demographic, economic and educational issues, and, most importantly, working on and managing conflict.[24,21]
5. *Improve the problem solving capabilities* of the partnership players by adopting a 'co-operative action research model of management'. This is a way of creating an action learning team whose main features include problem identification and analysis, a questioning approach, development of alternative solutions, action planning, project management and review.

It is appropriate for use on either specific or global issues and integrates the qualities of a 'think tank' into the organisational system.[25]

6. *Support the boundary workers* from all sectors of the partnership and encourage people from more organisations to venture into the no persons land which partnerships occupy. The boundary workers need to possess a conceptual understanding of consultation processes and practice. They will also need practical help in negotiating, contracting, motivating, implementing, reviewing and evaluating. The boundary workers should exhibit certain talents including entrepreneurial flair, a passion for partnerships, a commitment to communities in a broad sense, a willingness to take risks and an ability to think long-term and to engage in day to day tasks.[26]

7. *Develop operational and maintenance knowledge and skills.* In particular develop a cadre of internal change agents and consultants who can contribute to both individual organisational development and to the wider partnership scenario. This guideline is really a case of adopting the espoused partnership principles at a personal level on the basis of 'Do unto others as you would be done by'.[27]

8. *Establish in-house programmes of monitoring, reviewing and evaluating progress* which are economical, practical and effective so that quality can be assured. The evaluation needs to be quantitative and qualitative, formative and summative in nature and based on sound principles and approaches which relate to developing the human resource potential of the partnership.[28]

9. *Develop an information base* that constructs the partnership maps and helps partners orientate themselves and recognise the position of others. Give guidance about routes and connections through the map and remember that the map is not the territory.

10. *Run a sanity check,* preferably with disinterested critical friends across all these points and ask the questions: 'Does this action make sense?'; 'Will this progress partnership development?'; 'Who will this affect?'

Postscript

Some final notes of caution should be sounded about the effective management of partnerships since, just as there is a body of literature on managing organisations effectively, so there is evidence and a history of what can destabilise, demotivate and ultimately destroy partnerships. The principle of partnership has to be valued by the partners and if the partnership becomes a dumping ground for supernumary personnel from industry, education, the TEC or LEC it will fail. Partnerships attract people with vested interests who can be a force either for positive developments or stagnation. It is important to recognise that there are the evangelists and the obsessives who find partnership activity attractive. Beware the vandals and crazies!

There is great pressure on partnerships to make rapid progress by capitalising on current enthusiasm and commitment. In this charged atmosphere the creation of effective partnerships will depend upon the behaviour of all concerned. The management model is the partnership message and how people behave in their daily interactions, the attitudes they display, the feelings they engender to others, their levels of commitment and motivation and their ability to make things happen will all affect the quality of partnership activity.

This chapter began by asking readers to 'image' the partnership scenario from their own unique perspective. How does that landscape now look? Are the organisational forms enabling people's efforts? Is there a high degree of co-operation and collaboration? Are the relationships and communication patterns open, critical and supportive? Is there purpose, pride and quality in the community endeavours? Are the people being taken into account?

If the answers to these questions are negative then partnerships will have little of meaning or substance to offer communities and the nation as a whole. If the answers are positive, education business partnerships will flourish as central agencies in the regeneration of education and business.

References

1   Weick, K E, 1970, *The Social Psychology of Organizing*, Addison-Wesley.
2   Fayol, H 1949, *Industrial Management*, Pitman.
3. Maden, R, Gibbs, R E, et al, 1984, *Report of the Study Visit to the U.S.A. Investigating Aspects of School/Industry Activities for the 14-18 Age Range*, (unpublished).
4   Merenda, D, 1988, *The Practical Guide to Creating and Managing Partnerships*, National Association of Partnerships in Education, USA.

5   Argyris, C, Schon D A, 1978, *Organizational Learning: A Theory of Action Perspective*, Addision-Wesley.

6   Bennis, W G, Benne, K D, Chin R, 1984, *The Planning of Change*, Holt Rinehart Winston.

7   Mintzberg, H 1983, *Structure in Fives*, Prentice-Hall International.

8   Peters, T, 1989 *Thriving on Chaos*, Pan Books.

9   Peters, T J, Waterman, R H, 1982, *In Search of Excellence: Lessons from America's Best-run Companies*, Harper & Row.

10 Putnam, L, Pacanowsky, M E, 1983, *Communication and Organizations*, Sage.

11 Katz, D, Kahn, R L, 1978, *The Social Psychology of Organizations*, John Wiley.

12 Deal, T E, Kennedy, A A, 1982, *Corporate Cultures: The Rites and Rituals of Corporate Life*, Addison-Wesley.

13 Argyris, C, 1985, *Strategy, Change and Defensive Routines*, Pitman.

14 Taylor, F W, 1911, *Scientific Management*, Harper & Row.

15 Weber, M, 1948, *The Theory of Social and Economic Organization*, OUP.

16 Clough, E, Aspinwall, K, Gibbs, B, 1989, *Learning to Change*, Falmer.

17 Kreps,G L, 1990, *Organizational Communication*, Longman.

18 King, B, Lea, C, Moroney, G, 1991, *The Partnership Handbook*, Employment Department.

19 Handy, C, *Understanding Organizations*, Penguin.

20 Mumford A, 1986, *Handbook of Management Development*, Gower.

21 Pedler, M, Burgoyne, J, Boydell, T, 1988, *Applying Self-Development in Organizations*, Prentice-Hall.

22 Marsden, C, 1991, *Education and Business: a vision for the partnership*, BP.

23 Gibb, J R, 1961, Defensive Communication, *Journal of Communication*, 11.

24 Anthony, W P, Maddox, E N, Wheatley W Jnr, 1988, *A Guide for Human Resource Professionals in Management Training and Development*, Quorum.

25 Revans, R W, 1983, *The ABC of Action Learning*, Chartwell Bratt.

26 Schein, E H, 1969, *Process Consultation: Its Role in Organization and Development*, Addison-Wesley.

27 Lippitt, G, and Lippitt, R, 1986, *The Consulting Process in Action*, University Associates.

28 Patton, M Q, 1990, *Qualitative Evaluation and Research Methods*, Sage.

Fass, M, Scothorne, R, 1990, *The Vital Economy*, Abbeystrand.
Stewart, V, 1990, The David Solution, Gower.

Section II

Chapter 4: Partnership issues in the UK

Sean Lawlor and Andrew Miller

Introduction

The establishment of formal education-business partnerships is seen by many as the logical culmination of education-industry activity generated by the so-called schools-industry movement. Over the past two decades there has been a variety of such initiatives from central government, local education authorities, employers' organisations, the trade union movement, local employers and from teachers themselves. James Callaghan's Ruskin College speech of 1976 which launched the 'Great Debate' is generally regarded as a watershed. He drew attention to the lack of communication between schools and industry, and threw open the school curriculum to the wider community. The concerns expressed in the Ruskin speech were not new ones. They had been articulated in different forms since the mid-nineteenth century. What was new was the eagerness with which the gauntlet he threw down was picked up.

Following the speech, the Trade Union Congress (TUC) approached the Schools Council to initiate a project which would examine the role of trade unions in contemporary economic life. The Schools Council involved the Confederation of British Industry (CBI), and in 1978 the first Schools Council Industry Project (SCIP) co-ordinators were appointed in five local education authorities (LEAs). From its earliest days, SCIP placed the emphasis on local solutions to local problems. It resisted attempts to identify a body of knowledge which needed to be delivered about industry and developed a methodology based on learning through experience and the active involvement of adults-other-than-teachers (AOTs) in this learning process. It supported work experience and the development of simulations and case studies, and pioneered mini-enterprise in schools. From its local patches, SCIP has evolved into a national network covering most LEAs in England and Wales. SCIP provides one model of partnership in action, as its more recent name, School Curriculum Industry Partnership, implies. The Technical and Vocational Initiative (TVEI) was launched in 1982. TVEI was significant for a number of reasons. First the scheme was initiated by the Manpower Services Commission (MSC) which reported to the Department of Employment rather than the Department of Education and Science. Secondly, LEAs had to bid for funding and were awarded a contract to deliver their proposals. Progress was carefully monitored and evaluated at local and national level. Thirdly, TVEI was generously resourced (£240 million) at a time when education budgets were constrained. Finally, a specific 'cohort' of pupils had to be identified in each year group in the 14–19 age range, whose curriculum was to be enhanced by TVEI funding. Moreover, TVEI required schools and colleges to co-operate with each other and with employers in designing and delivering the TVEI curriculum.

Some LEAs and some teachers were concerned that TVEI represented an attempt to vocationalise the curriculum, and were reluctant to participate in the TVEI pilots. When the Government announced plans for extension in 1986, these fears were addressed by the requirements placed on LEAs to deliver TVEI within the framework of a 'broad, balanced and relevant' curriculum. In any case, changes in the way education is resourced, the enactment of the 1988 Education Reform Act and the implementation of the National Curriculum have overtaken such misgivings. TVEI has operated through local teams of teachers, often seconded for a fixed period. Such teams have two lines of management, one into the LEA they were serving, and the other into the Training Agency which was providing funding. Teams frequently include members with a brief for education-industry activity.

1986 was designated by the Royal Society of Arts (RSA) as Industry Year. In a publicity leaflet it was asserted that in Britain '... we hold industrial activity in low social esteem and the causes of our relative industrial decline are deeply embedded in our cultural attitudes'. Industry Year was a concerted attempt to raise the esteem in which industry was held. It concentrated therefore very often on public events — the holding of competitions, the hosting of award ceremonies. It worked through local committees bringing people from education and industry together, and it set for its goal that every school or college should have at least one activity or event in which people from the local education community were involved. In many areas of the country, it provided a much needed local forum for people from education and industry to come together. As the year drew to a close there was a recognition that the goodwill and co-operation generated should not be allowed to dissipate, and a newsletter *Industry Matters* was established to offer some continuing support for Industry Year committees.

The 1988 Employment White Paper Command 278 set out government policy on education and business, while the 'DTI - Department of Enterprise' White Paper established the DTI Enterprise and Education Initiative set out clear goals for pupils (100% work experience for eligible pupils), for teachers (10% of all teachers to be seconded to industry each year) and for initial teacher training. As a result of the DTI initiative two new players entered the education-industry arena, the DTI advisers, who were responsible for 'exciting industry about education', and more specifically supporting the achievement of goals for work experience and teacher secondment by ensuring that adequate placements were available, and the Teacher Placement Organisers (TPOs) managed via Understanding British Industry (UBI) who developed the teacher secondment to industry element.

The Cadbury Report 'Building Stronger Partnership Between Business and Secondary Education' (CBI, 1988) was addressed to industry and identified the economic importance of liaison with education. It drew attention to the 'alphabet soup' of education-industry initiatives and recommended that the education-industry partnership movement should be supported by a national body. This led to the establishment of the short-lived FEBP. One possible explanation for its demise is that there is so much activity promoted by initiatives, organisations and individuals, that its co-ordination by a single national body is not feasible.

Compacts, as launched by the MSC/Training Agency in 1988 were presented as '... a natural extension of the goal to promote the full potential of all young people through education and training so that they can take place as effective members of the nation's work force'. The 'Guidelines for MSC Support' document went on to define a Compact as:

> an agreement between employers and education. It evolves from a partnership between employers, schools and colleges, parents and young people, the Careers Service and community organisation. Having established common goals, the employers and education partners agree that all students who reach these goals and leave the schools and colleges in the COMPACT will be offered training and jobs.

One of the most significant aspects of Compact was its use of a formal agreement between education and industry to support agreed goals.

Further momentum was given to the schools-industry movement by the publication in 1989 of the CBI Vocational Education and Training Task Force Report 'Towards a Skills Revolution'. This report set our four broad objectives:

1) the establishment of 'world class' targets for training and education (e.g. by 1995 almost all young people should attain NVQ level II or its academic equivalent, i.e. five GCSEs at grade A-C and by the year 2000 half the age group should attain NVQ level III or its academic equivalent, i.e. two 'A' levels and five GCSEs at grade A-C;

2) the introduction of the concept of **Careership** to bridge the divide between education and training by introducing personal profiles supported by professional careers advice and support; providing 16 year olds with a cash credit 'to give them real buying power' in the education and training market; and offering more relevant transferable skills and broad based qualifications;

3) the insistence that all employers should become investors in training;

4) the establishment of a genuine **market** for training, through the introduction of individual training credits.

It addressed its recommendations to three distinct audiences: central government, employers and educationalists and identified a strategic role for TECs in carrying through the skills revolution it proposed.

Finally in 1990 following a statement in the House of Commons by Nicholas Ridley, the Secretary of State for Trade and Industry, the Training Agency published the *Education Business Partnership Prospectus* which was addressed primarily to Training and Enterprise Councils but required their proposals to receive the support of local education authorities.

The decade and a half from a Ruskin speech to the publication of the *Education-Business Partnership Prospectus* has seen significant changes in society and the expectations that society has from the education system. At the start of this period, the central position and key role of LEAs in planning and funding educational provision was indisputable, and it is not surprising that education-industry teams, often involving secondees from industry or personnel from government initiatives, should have developed within the LEA framework, and frequently appeared to work from the premise that education-industry activity would be initiated by education, and that industry would respond to the demands of education.

Industry Year, the DTI Enterprise and Education Initiative and MSC/Training Agency Compacts created for industry the possibility of a pro-active role. The purposes of education-industry liaison were open to question. While curriculum development retained a central role, the shaping of attitudes towards industry and wealth creation, meeting the needs of employers for a well-trained and motivated workforce and allowing employers to influence the shape of the whole curriculum began to assume greater importance. SCIP co-ordinators and members of the TVEI teams very often found their roles newly defined as members of inter-disciplinary teams working alongside people with a background in industry rather than education and with reporting structures which lay beyond the local authority framework. While these developments were often stimulating and challenging, they could also make for confusion about the means and purposes of industry/education activity: was it education **about** industry, education **for** industry or education **through** industry? How was achievement in the field to be measured? The setting of quantitative targets by the DTI for Work Experience and Teacher Secondments begged questions about quality. Was any work experience better than no work experience? What was the purpose of teacher secondment? Was teacher secondment necessarily the best way to achieve the ends achievement?

Different LEAs arrived at different solutions to these issues. Some brought together practitioners from different initiatives and established inter-disciplinary teams. Others made connections with other areas of LEA policy and practice: equal opportunity units, records of achievement pilots etc. A few pioneered new forms of education-industry interaction, such as Sheffield's Partnership Consultancy offering consultancy services to industry and to other LEAs, and Coventry's Partnership Centres which afford a bridgehead between education and industry through the establishment of learning centres on employers' premises.

Partnership study

In Autumn 1990, in anticipation of the publication of the *Partnership Prospectus*, SCIP commissioned a study of existing partnership activity. Of course, all education-industry activity requires a degree of partnership between education and industry, but, influenced by the definitions of partnership promulgated by the Federation for Education Business Partnerships (FEBP), SCIP were concerned to investigate 'system-wide' partnerships which exist at a level above that of individual educational institutions and operate within a formal constitutional framework with clearly stated measurable goals.

There were a number of goals which SCIP wished to investigate. First, it sought to establish what meanings practitioners attached to the term 'partnership' and what 'added value' they saw the establishment of a formal partnership bringing to their existing education-industry activities. Secondly, it wished to investigate how the partnerships had developed, who the partners and the clients were taken to be, and how partnerships related to the local labour market. Thirdly, it investigated the ways in which the partnerships were organised and the factors which had influenced these structures. Fourthly, it asked interviewees to define the key tasks and goals of the partnership in relation to the work of schools and colleges and to the needs of employers. Fifthly, it discussed the resource implications of partnerships (human, financial, accommodation, etc.). Finally it asked interviewees to define the major strengths of their partnerships and to share any problems or pitfalls.

The study was based on structured interviews conducted in five partnership areas. An interview schedule was prepared which covered the topics outlines above. A number of perspectives on each partnership were obtained: from employers; from teachers; from partnership personnel and from SCIP co-ordinators; and, depending on the way the partnership was organised from other personnel: from careers officers, TVEI co-ordinators, TPOs and DTI advisers. Literature and documents relating to the partnerships were also examined.

The five areas were chosen to provide a representative cross section of local authorities by geography, by size and by social character. Two were based on inner cities (Northchester and Newborough) which were participating in Training Agency funded Compacts, while three were based in shire counties (Southshire, Westshire, Eastshire). All of the LEAs were members of the SCIP network, and in most of them, SCIP co-ordinators played a central role in the partnership.

Meaning of partnership

The Government's *Education-Business Partnerships Prospectus* is addressed to Training and Enterprise Councils (TECs) and LEAs. The Prospectus recognises the way in which education and business have drawn together over the past decade and aims to 'build on the very solid foundation and to continue the momentum generated through activities such as the DTI's Enterprise and Education Initiative, Work Related Curriculum Programme, Inner City Compacts and TVEI'. The Prospectus enumerates a series of 'demonstrable outcomes':

- increased business involvement with, and support for, primary and secondary education;
- improved opportunities to assist students in school and college in the transition to work;
- increased volume, relevance and breadth of information and guidance offered to students by careers teachers and the Careers Service;
- increased number of young people staying in relevant and appropriate full-time and part-time education;
- improved access to, and participation to, further and higher education.

These outcomes are specifically concerned with transition education, and support for careers education in schools and colleges, and this emphasis is supported by the way in which funding is to be channelled through TECs.

The concept of partnership between education and industry was very important to everyone interviewed even if the meanings they derived from the term showed were at variance with the emphasis implied in the Prospectus. The education-industry adviser for Westshire argued that 'small is beautiful' and he defined partnership as any occasion where you have an educationalist and an industrialist working together. An employer in Eastshire argued for a relatively loose and informal structure. He did not believe that in general employers favoured formal, Compact-style agreements. The manager for one of the Westshire partnerships expressed the concern that the term 'education-business partnership' seemed to exclude elements of the wider community. While these concerns with the small, the informal and the broad, did not, however impede the establishment of formal partnerships covering the entire LEA (Northchester and Newborough) or a substantial area of it (Westshire, Southshire) they did give rise to some anxieties about the 'ownership' of partnership activities.

One way of addressing these anxieties is to explore who the partners actually are and who the clients are for partnership activity. There was a high degree of consensus on who the partners are in broad terms — anyone concerned with education and business has a stake in the partnership. At the organisational level this includes TECs and LEAs; at the institutional level, schools, colleges and individual companies; at the individual level teachers, students, parents, careers officers, employers, trade unionists and the whole community. Having identified the partners, most partnerships were in the process of drawing up representative structures. While employers were recognised as significant clients for partnership activities, the principle client was perceived as the individual pupil or student. Some interviewees argued that all the partners were potential or indirect clients.

Taking this broader view, many of the interviewees saw a programme of economic and industrial understanding, spanning all phases of education, as a means of promoting the demonstrable outcomes proposed in the Prospectus, and they could see an enabling role for partnerships in delivering the programme. They emphasised continuity between the goals of partnership work linking education and industry that had already been achieved, but there were concerns that partnerships might not have sufficient resources to continue funding initiatives such as TVEI and the DTI Education and Enterprise Programme as government funding tails off. This concern was especially acute in relation to the labour-intensive organisational tasks, such as managing work experience and teacher secondment to industry, which have tended to be managed centrally, and which are identified in the *Partnership Prospectus* as key tasks within the detailed action plan which is required to obtain operational funding.

Compact and partnership

The 'Guidelines for MSC Support' described a Compact as '... (evolving) from a partnership between employers; schools and colleges, parents and young people; the Careers Service and community organisations'. In most cases, however, there was no formal partnership structure for Compact to build on. In Newborough and Northchester Compact stimulated the development of a formal partnership. In Northchester, Compact is managed within the partnership framework. In Newborough, parallel directorates have been established for Partnership and Compact while Southshire (which was not an Urban Programme Area) has adapted the Compact model in establishing its partnership.

Compacts were established to address a set of economic and social policy problems — to answer the needs of employers in inner cities for a well-motivated and multi-skilled workforce, and to win worthwhile employment opportunities for young people from disadvantaged backgrounds. Their distinctive feature is the Compact guarantee, the offer of a job with training, or training leading to a job, for all young people who reach certain goals. The job offer, originally, pitched at the 16 year old school leaver, and the Compact qualification was expressed in terms of personal qualities (attendance, punctuality) and life skills, rather than in terms of educational achievement. The English and mathematics qualification reflect an emphasis on basic competencies rather than an incentive to raise achievement. Thus although Compacts were intended to be founded on an existing partnership the process has in many instances been reversed. There is little doubt that the Compacts have had a strong influence on many developing partnerships.

Role and function

The Education-Business Partnership Prospectus sets out the broad aims of education-business partnerships:

> Partnerships between education and business offer opportunities to make education more relevant to life and work; to raise standards and levels of attainment, to raise enterprise awareness and industrial understanding amongst teachers and students, and to inform and develop advice and counselling so that individuals are better placed to build and use their skills.

It recognises that the progress that has been made in bringing education and business closer together, and seeks to build on this foundation. It recognises that the specific aims of each partnership will reflect local conditions while stressing that all partnerships should have an agreed set of strategic objectives which should be 'clear, achievable, timebound and measurable' representing the 'agreed, shared aims of the partners' and reflecting 'the value which is added by organisations working collaboratively rather than independently.'

The role of partnerships as essentially representative and co-ordinating bodies emerged clearly from our study of the five partnership areas. Two key aspects of the role were identified:

1. Co-ordinating or organising activities such as work-experience, mock interviews, and teacher secondment to industry, by providing a contact point for education and business partners, embodying the concept of 'one-stop shopping';

2. Stimulating or promoting innovation, by sharing good practice and improving communication between education and
   business partners.

'One-stop shopping' had been achieved in three of the five partnerships, by providing shared accommodation for schools-
industry professionals (e.g. SCIP co-ordinators, work-experience
co-ordinators, DTI advisers and TPOs). The benefits flowing
from such an arrangement included teambuilding and the promotion of a common vision as well as administrative conve-
nience. Conflicts which might otherwise have arisen through
diverging lines of management had been avoided.

It was also recognised, however, that the co-ordination role is a
partial and provisional one. There was evidence in all partnerships of activities which, while they might fly the partnership
flag, had not been instigated by the central partnership team.
Typically, they arose from an independent approach (usually
school to employer, in one case, employer to school) or were a
development from an activity, such as teacher secondment to
industry, which had been initiated by a member of the partnership team. There was a marked difference too, in the extent of
central co-ordination between densely populated urban areas
where schools are relatively close together and employers more
susceptible to a multitude of approaches, and rural areas where
the population, and hence schools and businesses, are relatively
sparse. In the inner cities, for example, co-ordination of work-
experience is seen as essential, whereas in rural areas it may be
best managed at individual school level.

People in all the partnerships studied were aware of areas for
potential partnership innovation. These included promoting
industry-education work with primary schools, improving support for core and foundation studies in the National Curriculum
and for economic and industrial understanding and careers education. Northchester had organised schools into 'pyramids'
where primary schools, secondary schools and employers come
together to develop education-industry initiatives.

Structure and organisation

There are three clear elements which contribute to the structure
of partnerships: representation, management and activity. In
some ways securing appropriate representation is the most
elusive element. Eastshire has a well established Forum, which
provides a meeting place for all with an interest in education-
industry work. It sponsors a range of activity and elects an

annual council to oversee progress. Other partnerships have held conferences based on schools (Northchester), TVEI consortia (Southshire and Westshire) or workshops involving employers, educationalists and parents and young people (Newborough) to enable all interested parties to be represented. Despite such attempts, participants in all five partnership areas identified the representation of all stakeholders as partners as an enormous, difficult and challenging task.

Most of the partnerships studied had developed a three-tier management structure. Although there was considerable variation in the terms used the characteristics of these three tiers, which we may call Partnership Council, Executive Committee and Management and Operational Team, were reasonably clear:

• *The Partnership Council* has a symbolic role. Its members are drawn from the great and the good. It says to the local community that partnership is important. Members may well have been the signatories of the charter that established the partnership, as in Northchester. The council is unlikely to meet very often or to exert much control over day-to-day activity. Westshire was developing four area partnerships based on the local authorities administrative divisions. When these are established consideration will be given to the creation of an over-arching body for the county. At present, it does not have a Partnership Council layer.

• *The Executive Committee* is charged with overseeing the operation of the partnership. It may well set targets and decide on priorities. It is the body that partnership managers report to, and they will usually attend its meetings. It is generally seen as important that industry and education have roughly equal representation on this group. In some cases this has led to executives which were considered too large to be effective by some of the interviewees. In Northchester, a desired reduction in size was achieved by splitting the committee into two: an executive and an advisory group. Education is represented on the executive by LEA officers and inspectors, while college principals and school heads are members of the advisory group.

• *The Management and Operational Team* is the engine that drives the partnership. It may consist solely of the partnership manager and a personal assistant, as in Southshire, although this is unusual. It is more likely to consist of an education manager and a business manager supported by other personnel with a responsibility for specific areas of work, (e.g. DTI adviser, SCIP co-ordinator, TPO). Such people are unlikely to be employed directly by the partnership.

The management and operational team is responsible for the delivery of the partnership's activities. It works closely on a day-to-day basis with employers and schools and colleges. There are potentially some problems with this arrangement. First, the support personnel (DTI advisers, TPOs, SCIP co-ordinators) have separate management lines to their funding organisations or the LEA. Their contribution to the partnership has to be negotiated. This was a satisfactory process in all the areas we studied. Secondly, some personnel were on fixed term contract (e.g. DTI advisers) or threatened by redundancy. Questions were raised about the ability of partnerships to deliver the range of activity that is currently taking place. Some of the partnerships are looking to TECs and employers for replacement funding, while others are looking to income-generating enterprises, such as Northchester's consultancy or Newborough's sponsored careers convention.

Goals and their formulation

The partnerships approached the construction of their goals in a variety of ways. Southshire borrowed its goals from a Compact and adapted these to its partnership. Pupil goals, for example, includes 95% attendance and 95% punctuality, as well as goals relating to coursework deadlines, work experience, sitting examinations and literacy and numeracy. Employers agree to priority consideration for interview selection and placement to students who have achieved their personal goals. They make a commitment to equal opportunities, quality training, supporting students with special needs and the development of schools and industry link activities.

In Northchester and Newborough the development of partnership is closely related to the introduction of Compact. In Northchester, the local youth employment market was such that a guaranteed job for all Compact goal achievers was undeliverable, and the Youth Training programme was already making a significant contribution to post-school provision. This led to the concept of a broad partnership between education and industry, open to all, and embracing a Compact which all secondary and tertiary institutions could join. Specific goals within the partnership related to Compact. The goals for individual schools and colleges include:

- the provision of work-related experience for all students

- the development of a RoAE (Record of Achievement and Experience) for each student, in formative and summative forms
- the involvement of a wide representation from the community in the validation of the RoAE
- provision for the professional development of staff in business environments
- the provision of an enhanced guidance package for students, including:
  — a review of personal goals and progress
  — self presentation skills
  — access to advice from partnership employers;
  — an underlining of the importance of a committed approach to learning.

The goals for individual students include:

- commitment to agreed learning programmes
- demonstration of their achievements against personal targets
- participation in work experience/work related experience
- completion of a RoAE.

The emphasis is on the setting of challenging but achievable targets for the individual student.

Employers make a general commitment to support the Compact and in particular: to undertake collectively to support strategies promoting training and career development opportunities for all students who graduate from the Compact programme; to use their influence to secure sufficient good quality training and employment opportunities for Compact graduates; and, where possible, to offer Compact jobs.

In addition, the partnership has a three-fold mission as outlined in the original contract:

1. To improve both partners knowledge and understanding of the other's work, philosophy and needs.
2. To work together to improve the standard of labour market information available to the city and to ensure that education and training become more responsive to the likely demands for skills.
3. To seek to improve the relevance of young people's educational experience in schools and colleges to the demands of the world of work.

The Newborough partnership developed its Compact goals through workshops. They were organised early in the developmental phase to initiate and establish the planning and consultation process. Key partners with more or less equal representation were drawn from:

• *Employers:* representatives from a range of business sectors, small and large companies. Newborough Council, the Local Employer Network (LEN), TEC Development Group.

• *Education:* headteachers, senior managers representing all secondary schools, special schools and the college.

• *Parents and young people:* representatives from parent/governor organisations; young people aged 14, 15, 16 and 17 from school and YTS.

Other partners involved in the workshops included the Training Agency, executive directors, LEA officers and inspectors, Careers Service, trade unions, DTI advisers, TVEI co-ordinators and Compact directorate.

In Eastshire the partnership's goals are expressed through the annual workplan negotiated between the director of the Forum and his line manager in education. In Westshire, which is establishing four area partnerships based on local authority divisions, each partnership is constructing its own goals:

• To improve the opportunities for young people to achieve suitable employment opportunities with the appropriate education and development.

• To encourage employers to articulate clearly their expectations of young people in such a way that it can helpfully inform the curriculum in schools and colleges.

• To provide a forum where eduction and industry can work together to create a better range of provision in education and training.

• To assist young people in the progression from full time-education to full-time employment.

• To raise understanding in businesses, schools, colleges and amongst parents of what local business and education are trying to do, and to reduce misunderstanding and suspicion.

• To bring coherence (but not centralisation) to existing links between education and industry.

• To generate resources and funding to enable these objectives to be achieved.

• To promote and market these activities with a view to gaining the widest possible degree of involvement from business, education, parents, and the wider community.

N.B. These objectives are modelled on those of existing partnerships elsewhere.

The consortium did not seek to construct goals for individual pupils on the Compact model.

An employer's liaison group in another division produced the following objectives:

1. To improve the links between employers and local schools and colleges:
   - to co-ordinate the various employers work in the area through the Chamber of Commerce, LENs, Industry Matters and others
   - to provide regular contact between representatives of industry and education in order that co-ordination can be maintained.
2. To provide a forum in which information relevant to local employers and the education service can be freely exchanged:
   - to allow for debate on key educational initiatives such as the development of GCSE, TVEI and the National Curriculum so that employer representatives can be properly briefed
   - to provide information, for the benefit of educationalists, on training schemes for young people in which employers are involved
   - to provide an opportunity for employers to bring in teacher representatives regarding any research and surveys they may undertake through agencies such as the LENs
   - to provide feedback on work experience from both the schools' and colleges' points of view and also that of the employers.
3. To give an opportunity for local employers to comment on and become involved in curricular development in schools and colleges:
   - to support the work of employer representatives on local TVEI management committees
   - to encourage employers to contribute to the learning of young people by becoming involved in the classroom
   - to provide a means whereby employers can debate and contribute to the Record of Achievement
   - to promote and develop the careers curriculum in schools and colleges in order to provide a good information and advice service for young people entering employment and/or training schemes.

The education-industry adviser for Westshire emphasised that it was the process of coming together to formulate goals, with the exchange of opinion, information and insight that that involves, which is most important. The goals themselves are less important. They can be refined and improved over time. The 'ownership' of the goals by each of the four partnerships was essential, and there is no intention, therefore, at present to attempt to create goals for the county as a whole.

Personnel issues

Existing partnerships have drawn their operational teams from three principle sources: from existing LEA staff with an education-industry brief (e.g. SCIP co-ordinators); from personnel associated with other government initiatives (e.g. TPOs, DTI advisers); and from managers seconded by industry, although all three sources are not necessarily represented within each partnership. In Southshire, for example, the partnership manager, seconded from industry, works in collaboration with TVEI consortia in the partnership area but he does not have an identifiable team. Local conditions mean that it is most unlikely that all partnership staff will be provided by education; any additional staff would have to come also from industry. In the area partnerships in Westshire, education managers had been appointed to three divisions, while a business manager had been seconded in the fourth. It is proposed that each division should have co-managers from education and industry. Eastshire has an education director for its Forum for Industry and Education (which is seen as a partnership vehicle) who works closely with the DTI adviser and the TPO. There is no business manager. Northchester and Newborough have more clearly identified partnership teams, with joint managers from education and industry and teams involving a full range of other personnel. The concentration of population, and, therefore, of resources in urban areas makes this sort of team a possibility.

Partnership teams include people from a variety of backgrounds and areas of expertise. LEA staff with a teaching background can be expected to have skills in curriculum innovation. They are likely through their experience of education-industry co-ordination to have developed a high level of negotiating skill and to have a feeling for local issues. Some partnerships (e.g. Northchester, Newborough and Westshire have recognised this and have promoted these key personnel and redesignated them as partnership education managers to ensure that they have a status equivalent to partnership managers seconded from industry. The introduction of Local Management of Schools (LMS), however, raises questions about the continuing ability of LEAs to afford to fund such posts. Teachers moving to such posts also face an uncertain future in career development terms.

Some personnel who have been inherited by partnerships from other initiatives, may be moving from a relatively narrowly-defined role such as the management and resourcing of a work-experience database, to a broader sphere of activity. Where this is the case, the partnership needs to consider their training and career development needs.

Business managers are usually selected by the companies which are seconding them. Two distinct approaches can be recognised. Some secondments are viewed as part of the professional development of younger managers, who will return to their firms after a period of two years or so, very often to more senior positions. Other secondments are viewed as part of a pre-retirement package for older managers, who may possibly continue to work with the partnership after retirement. There are examples of effective training as managers from both categories. In some partnerships, companies have been assisted in selecting appropriate personnel by the negotiation of a clear job description and person specification by the partnership body. The education-industry adviser for Westshire pointed out that no matter how skilled any business manager may be, a steep learning curve has to be negotiated by any secondee. The need for a structured induction programme had therefore been identified in a number of partnerships.

As LEAs reorganise their administrative and advisory structures in response to LMS and government sponsored initiatives, such as the DTI Education and Enterprise Programme, draw to a close, partnerships have to find ways of closing the gap that the departure of key personnel such as SCIP co-ordinators and DTI advisers will leave. Strategies include seeking replacement funding from other sources (industrial sponsorship), marketing partnership services to generate income, and re-prioritising partnership activities.

Conclusion

It was apparent in our study of the five partnership areas that although the establishment of the Federation of Education Business Partnerships (FEBP) and the publication of the *Prospectus for Education-Business Partnerships* had given a new impetus to partnership initiatives, partnership between education and industry was in itself not a new concept. It might reasonably be traced back, in its current form, to the inception of SCIP and other initiatives in the late 1970s. There were, however, a number of features of partnership which were new, or which had been given a new emphasis.

First there was a widespread interest in the establishment of partnership structures. While these have a practical role in initiating new and co-ordinating existing activities, they also, very often, have an important symbolic role, in representing the commitment of business and education to work together. There is often a concern to reflect this commitment by ensuring equality of representation within the partnership structure. Many of the partners interviewed emphasised the importance of 'ownership' of the partnership by all involved, but there was some difficulty in distinguishing appropriate means of promoting ownership at different levels, e.g. the strategic, the executive and the operational. Individual teachers and employers, for example, who might be actively working together in the education-industry field, do not necessarily see their co-operation as a partnership activity. Some practitioners perceived a danger in partnership committees becoming 'talking shops' rather than 'action stations', while others feared the growth of partnership bureaucracies.

Secondly, recent changes in the structure and funding of education and training make for an uncertain future for established partnerships. In four of the five partnership areas a number of key personnel, including partnership managers were employed by a local authority, and accommodation was provided in local authority premises. There have been redundancies in all four areas, with the Newborough partnership most directly affected. Partners had looked to the government's partnership initiative and to TECs to replace funding no longer available to LEAs, but there is widespread concern that in the meantime, much existing good practice may be lost.

There was widespread agreement that the needs of young people and employers were likely to be best served by a broadly based partnership which valued the contributions of all partners, whether from education, industry or the wider community.

Chapter 5: Partnership and the flight from fancy: the promotion of partnership policy in higher education

Harry Gray

There is a very long tradition of collaboration between education and employers that stretches back to the foundation of the Mechanics Institutes in the nineteenth century — and to their even earlier precursors the Dissenting Academies — and developing through the technical colleges, colleges of advanced technology, technological universities and colleges of further and higher education. In some areas the link with professional employment was integral to the courses taught — teacher and medical education exemplify this *par excellence* — but employers have never been very far away from the design and validation of courses in the 'public sector'. In some urban areas the link with local employers — usually the major local employer — was exceedingly close as with mining colleges (Castleford and Camborne) or the steel industry (Scunthorpe and Rotherham). There were also apprentice schools attached to large manufacturers such as the Metropolitan-Vickers Apprentice School in Trafford Park, Manchester, which offered a dedicated form of secondary education for apprentices with that large electrical engineering firm, some of whom would also in due course seek employment with other electrical manufacturers.

But these relationships may not have been partnerships in any of the senses that the word is used today. The appropriate words may have been sponsorship, influence or control but whatever they were they were bound up very much in local politics. As such they have to be understood with nuances of influence and control often benign but sometimes narrow in focus. Partnership is a more recent concept and it would not fit in too well with the motivations which inspired early industrialists' and educationalists' interest in further and higher education.

Levels of partnership

Partnership is an easy word to use carelessly, particularly in the context of education and community activity. If we look carefully we shall see that there are three levels (or, since there is a progression over time, they may be called 'phases') of partnership. They achieve different things and they probably represent a hierarchy of development or an historical sequence. They may be identified by the nature of the relationship that they involve and be termed 'gift', 'exchange', and 'synergistic'. The first level — the gift relationship — is characterised by an inequality in the relationship such as sponsorship where a firm offers an institution something with no direct or equivalent return. It may provide a school with a sports strip, probably indicating sponsorship by having the firm's name on clothing, or donate some surplus machinery to a college. Or they may even spend a good sum of money on refurbishing a suite of rooms with no apparent requirement of reward other than perhaps the naming of the rooms in acknowledgement. There has been a lot of this kind of partnership in recent years and there is no doubt that there is some mutual benefit but the benefits are unrelated for each party — the college gets a resource that it can use, the donor a warm sense of public spirit, a tax deduction or some publicity. There may even be considerable altruism on the part of the donor, particularly where a member of the family is also a student in the institution. In this first level relationship, the educational institution may seek out gifts or they may be unsolicited but the relationship essentially involves the giving and receiving of gifts.

The second level of partnership — the exchange relationship — is characterised by a more direct connection between what a donor or sponsor offers and what the institution offers in return. There is an up front awareness of an exchange — if you provide us with typewriters we will place your company logo on our notepaper for a year. There may be considerable bargaining in this process and the educational institution may positively seek sponsors who can be persuaded into an exchange. Sponsors, too, may actively seek out educational institutions to see if some working arrangement can be made — the testing of a product or its promotion. There may be other more altruistic motives such as the sponsor being the largest employer in the town and this being one way of expressing community concern. A more sophisticated form of level two is the coalition, where partners work together for some common purpose but do not have an identity of interest or concern and where one or other of the partners may withdraw leaving the other partner(s) to continue. Most of the current partnerships in further and higher education (FHE) are of this nature, even if the inter-relationships of the parties are complicated, even complex, because the employer contribution usually relates to the financial state of the firm and this may change abruptly. In education operational time scales tend to be longer than commercial ones, certainly so far as joint projects are concerned.

Levels one and two are by far the commonest in education but there is a new type of partnership which appears to be developing and which may meet the needs of the future rather more fully than the other two — though those will always continue in existence because they fulfil real short term needs. The third level is one of interdependence and mutual growth and development, of synergy. In this relationship there is active involvement, collaboration and co-operation during the whole process of the relationship in an enterprise that neither party could achieve on their own. This is not a symbiotic relationship because that involves a continuing separateness of identity throughout the period and process of partnership but it is an integrated relationship in which the enterprise — venture or project or more general association — is on a level of continued mutuality of interest and concern. Each party receives a reward that is dependent on the reward the other parties receive; there is a common interest. At this level the educational institution and the employer undertake something that neither could or would undertake on their own and which enhances the viability of each partner in their own normal sphere of activity and in their shared and mutual environment, community or market place. Such partnerships cannot succeed unless there is institutional commitment to partnership; it is not enough simply for individuals to work together.

Who are the partners?

There is, however, the problem of who the working partners actually are, especially at level three. Are they institutions and organisations, or representatives of institutions and organisations, or individuals who are members of institutions and organisations who are acting independently? Are they delegates, representatives or plenipotentiaries, for instance? And are their loyalties to their parent organisation, or to the host organisation, or to both? The question of institutional support is important but this is sometimes stronger in its rhetoric than its substance. In any case, organisations can only be represented by their members, and in partnerships it is individuals who are the active partners. These individuals act both personally — that is, both as the kinds of people they are, and representationally — that is, with those powers and permissions that others in the organisation allow them. Being a representative of a corporation is difficult and partly dependent on status within the corporate body. Top managers tend to be more closely identified with corporate policy than lower level representatives. A top level representative may be able to decide policy without reference to anyone else but others will have to refer back for an opinion on key matters. And there is also a problem of continuity; the original negotiating partners may not be the ones who continue and the successors may have different, even conflicting, motives.

A possible moral dilemma

One of the operational difficulties is whether the individuals have a primary loyalty to the venture or to their own employing organisation. Much will depend on the kind of organisation for which they work; some employers and educational institutions are more open and liberal than others. Some more ready to change; others more conservative or protective of themselves. There are important ethical issues here. Sometimes where there is a third party, such as a foundation with clear principles or there is government or local authority involvement, the pressure on the foundation representatives and public servants is to conform to an 'official' position which may be at odds with the way the project is developing and the views of the other partners. In any living venture, it is impossible for any of the partners to be detached from the natural dynamics of working together in the project and there may have to be a realignment of membership during the course of the enterprise. Sometimes the third party may have to withdraw because the process goes beyond the statutory obligations laid upon it but this will raise questions about its integrity which are not easy to answer.

There are often more substantial resources behind partners from large industrial companies than their partners from educational institutions. One of the more obvious characteristics of partnerships has been that educational partners are generally the poor relation — at least they usually behave as if they are — probably because partnerships are measured essentially in terms of cash rather than other kinds of resource such as accommodation, talent, expertise, knowledge and creativity. Industrial partners often have a budget allowed specifically for the operation of the partnership and of more generous proportions than budgets allowed to educationists. There may be a greater sense of adventure and novelty for employer partners than education partners because they are moving into a new field and are relieved of some of the responsibilities of their old job. But this can also be true of educationalists who are seconded to a new project outside their own institution. Novelty often provides good motivation.

Behind the active partners, there is the organisation — the firm of institution — and the dependency of the partnership on broader considerations in the parent body. In partnerships at levels one and two, the parent body may pull the plug or change the terms of reference because the partnership activity is not essential to the main business of the company. But in level three partnerships, the identity of interest is within the core business — or vision perspective — of the partners and withdrawal would involve a diminution of activity in the life-sustaining activity of all the partners. That is why the new partnerships can only be understood in terms of the contemporary concepts of organisational mission and vision.

The old tradition

The old tradition of partnership between employers and education was based on two not necessarily complementary assumptions. One was that education had an increasingly vocational function especially at post-elementary level and the other was a vague notion that 'education is a good thing and therefore ought to be supported'. There has always been an unresolved tension in the English and Welsh educational systems between the view that education is broad and general while training is specific and vocational. The dysfunctional force of this distinction between education and training has been reinforced by the binary system of state and public schools and by the belief in a 'classic' non-vocational education as a gold standard or jewel in the crown against which other educational activity is pejoratively judged. It is still present in the uncertainty in the second sector about 'traditional values' in education and the desire within some parents — and some teachers — for schooling that is essentially instructional and didactic.

The two related factors that have worked against an integration of education and training have been traditional recruitment into the professions via Oxbridge, and the view that the *summum bonum* of English education is A levels. Together these viewpoints have distorted the development of English education at the expense of a balanced provision in a system which could be expected to be concerned with the broad world of personal development, preparation for employment and providing for economic and community need, both local and national. It is for these reasons that levels one and two of partnership have been more prevalent than level three. The effect has been to deny the right of employers to a proper say in the educational process because their interest has been confined to recruitment after the event rather than as participants in provision. The public school plus Oxbridge system has never perceived any need for vocational education and consequently it has been denied to the student body at large.

Traditional activities in co-operation

Of course, there are other complications in the situation. Perhaps the most important of these has been that public education in England and Wales has been a service provided by public local authorities and paid for out of taxes. Higher education — for the most part — has been an extension of this system whereby education is largely autonomous of commerce and industry, and employer contributions have been almost entirely supplementary and subordinate to state provision. That is not to deny the wide range of activities that have involved employers. Some employers sponsor students by paying fees and maintenance; there is widespread employer involvement in various forms of sandwich courses and work placements including, in some cases, co-operation in student assessment; there are endowed chairs at universities and polytechnics; there are sponsored courses sometimes with a single client as customer for the whole student cohort; employers sit on various boards and committees concerned with activities from course unit level to governing body; employers use academics as consultants and engage academic departments to do research for them; there are sponsored research and collaborative projects; and curriculum material is available at all levels — usually for free — from industrial and commercial bodies.

The institutions offer a service in that they train graduates whom many large employers and some small ones recruit, often on the basis of a degree — content, quality and grade. Employers may find that supporting educational institutions is good for their public image and even direct advertising. There may be economies in using higher educational facilities as locations for events and academics as consultants; and some of these resources may be cheaper than they would be if the company had to provide them as a call on the payload. But it can hardly be said that the relationship between the two sectors has been as mutually productive as it might be. Employers have until recently been kept at arms' length and away from sensitive areas of involvement within academic institutions, including management. And it is certain that the development of level three partnerships is dependent upon not just a rethinking by the sector partners but by government and its role in education and training — a process which has undoubtedly begun, but in a fitful a way and without truly fundamental thinking. We may have to await reports from the British Association and the Royal Society of Arts, the Engineering Fellowship and other bodies before the necessary sea change occurs.

New vision

Since it will be a long time before the reflective process turns into action plans, we shall have to make do with what we already know and for the purposes of this chapter we can relate it to Level Three Partnership. Thinking about past achievement and its relevance to the future has already begun. The present state of affairs in higher education is one of considerable flux. It is a period of constant, but intermittent, reflection and re-examination of essential roles and purposes with a questioning of past practices by those both within the institutions and those without, particularly the large international companies. There are two broad areas to be addressed — they are the nature of the mission of institutions and companies in each of the sectors and the character of vision that is an extension of clarity in business purpose.

One of the more encouraging features of the modern international corporation or organisation is the careful consideration of its mission followed by an assessment of its broad social and economic role as an extension of basic mission. International companies try increasingly to evolve a global vision in which their core economic activities are seen in a wider socio-economic context. No longer can a company survive simply in terms of immediate market pressures but only in terms of an international market place and the general and well distributed creation of wealth. Of course, there are often political reasons why this vision cannot yet be fully realised but that is all the more reason why an understanding should be pursued. The consolidation of Europe after 1992 into a coherent socio-economic unit will facilitate the process of defining the relationship between mission and vision. Presumably on a world scale this will also occur within the different economic blocks — North America, Pacific Rim, Soviet Union or whatever.

A third partner

In this new view of partnership, there will undoubtedly be a third partner — or group of partners; government and private agencies such as foundations and associations. They will act in a facilitating role to help in focusing on more general social and economic need. One of the problems with economic cycles is that they create surpluses and slacks in demand which affect the stability of the work force. The traditional role of governments in the UK has been to ease the pressures on both companies and individuals by some form of intervention — subsidies, loans or payments etc. In recent years the Employment Department and the Department of Trade and Industry have been responsible for appropriate interventions but they have been more of a fire fighting nature than a sustained development of policy and role — which in any case, has not been the way government departments have tended to behave since they are organised to implement government policy in the immediate rather than long term. Now the role of these third-parties must change to being of a more sustained nature as facilitators in long term policy and strategy for each major industry.

To do this, education has to be seen as a continuing life process linked to social and economic activity at all points and not just as a precurser to employment and a dependent adjunct thereafter. Education and employment need to be seen as but facets of the life process — that is of the learning process. Work and education will be integrated and 'employment' — that is, the duality of learning and working — will be a social and economic activity for which commerce and industry, educational institutions, and government with assistance from foundations will work in tripartite partnership. In some of the large international companies this process of amalgamating mission and vision has already begun — though it can, of course be traced back to the philanthropic industrialists of the eighteenth and nineteenth centuries. Today, for example, in Unilever, employees over the age of fifty may choose to work progressively less with the firm and more with the community until in their last year before retirement they work only one day a week with the firm. DEC (Digital) will only work with educational institutions if the project is of advantage to the broader community and not just for the benefit of the school or college. Other international companies are moving in the same direction and many, like ICI and BP, are firmly committed in principle to community regeneration.

Smaller companies

The weakness of employer partnerships has always lain with smaller firms, though many of them have been quite strong in the gift relationship offering small goodies in times of prosperity. In public rhetoric small companies have often been lumped together with the large internationals and the same expectations have been imposed. Yet many small and medium companies cannot give very much in the way of resources and may be in need of a great deal for themselves. Education has learned to grab with ease but not to reach out and yet there is a good deal of help that can be given to small businesses and voluntary organisations once the idea of level three partnership has been grasped. Many small companies could be sustained over difficult periods in their life-cycle if they were associated with caring educational institutions who could offer facilities, skills training, professional consultancy, sharing of staff on a flexible give and take basis, students seconded as real working additions to the work force, joint economic ventures such as trading, shared facilities such as crêches, and so on. Level three partnership works both ways and in every way and each potential partner has to discover and learn the skills appropriate to its place in the partnership.

Rethinking the mission of higher education

There is a great responsibility for higher education — that is, each individual institution as well as the service at large — to rethink its own mission and vision. Quite independent of the way higher eduction may be funded, there is a need for higher education institutions to rethink their role and function just as much as it behoves industry, commerce and the public services. Education is an economic activity in more ways than one. For one thing, people are employed and suppliers engaged; money changes hands in the local economy. For another students are customers both of the institution and local services. Education itself provides enrichment to the lives of individuals in a number of ways and in so doing determines the quality of life made possible by wealth creation. Indeed, education itself has an added value that is a form of wealth creation. Where educational institutions work in partnership with other bodies, they add to the vitality of the region and bring energy to economic regeneration. To do this, the 'vocational' element in eduction is critical because it increases the skills people have for use in a variety of enterprises; it allows people to make use of their learning.

There are many ways in which educational institutions can increase their involvement with society at large and become a potent force in social and economic regeneration. But few of them can be done in isolation and all require some element of partnership. Once employers and educationalists take as given the need to look beyond themselves and their own internal interests, there will be the possibility of a braver and newer world, that is more humanitarian and more caring. This world will be different from the one we know by being both more educated, better trained and more utilitarian, characterised by greater economic growth and social responsibility. It will be both a richer world and a less expensive one. It will be a world in which people and organisations learn and grow. It will be a world in which individuality is better respected and social consciousness is more mature. Above all it will be a society where people have learned how to learn; a truly learning society.

Acknowledgement

My thanks are due particularly to Gus Pennington and Lorraine Baric for their comments which have helped to clarify my ideas and emphasis.

Chapter 6: Partnerships 16–19: possibilities and pitfalls

Michael Austin

There is an assumption, current and beguiling, that education-industry partnerships are a 'Good Thing' for the 16–19 sector. Like similar assumptions about fresh air and freedom it needs further investigation, otherwise we shall measure its extent rather than its quality, its coverage rather than its benefits.

What, then, is meant by a partnership in this context? If it is not of mutual benefit it is no partnership at all, more a relationship of a parasite to host. It may well be that many apparently successful partnerships continue only because one party or the other does not trouble to examine the benefit they derive or the price they pay. It may be that, for them, a warm glow of public-spirited righteousness or a curriculum with work-experience, injected like silicone into a misshapen body, are sufficient reward. We need to do better than that, and we can. So what is partnership for?

From the point of view of the school or college there could be a number of more or less tangible advantages. They would include: opportunities for students to see or experience equipment or processes which are not on offer within the institution; the chance for a student to sample a possible future job or career; the opportunity to learn something (not much) of the lives led in employment by their neighbours, their parents or their peer-group, so that they may grow up more understanding and more tolerant (this rather pious hope may in fact be quite unjustified, they may have confirmed or developed disdain or envy for others); a good student may catch the eye of an employer looking for a later recruit; absence may lend enchantment to the view of the college and the students may return from work-experience reassured about their choice of education; students may be motivated to work hard at college by the prospect of either securing a job like the one they have seen or tried, or by the determination to avoid a similar fate; all these outcomes may be little more predictable than the consequences of going to the zoo for a visit. All these examples pre-suppose, without justification, that for a school or college partnership means work-experience. But it often does, and little or nothing else.

But there are other manifestations which, properly planned and resourced, can and do yield well. The support and guidance of 'real' employers on the boards of mini enterprise schemes can be helpful; the advice of professionals about equipment purchase, attendance-pattern of trainees, syllabus choice or, even, staff recruitment can all be derived from an active and effective pattern of Governors' Advisory Committees; industrial or commercial figures on governing bodies can give a helpful perspective; one-off lectures or presentations on an aspect of the business world can enhance a course — but all these examples depend for their success on agreed objectives. The dangers of institutions listening too much to special-interest pleading are self-evident; a badly-presented contribution from a visiting speaker can damage the image of a whole industry; hijacking of governors' meetings by self-important and opinionated individuals is an alienating experience, irrespective of whether the offender is an educationalist or an industrialist.

So, it is necessary to define objectives, plan for them, and monitor progress. In these tasks precision is important. An objective for a partnership of 'bringing industry and education closer together' is worse than useless, it is dangerously vague as to meaning and intention. Worthwhile objectives can be expected only after a listing of what each partner could bring to a relationship.

This might be, from the school/college side:

- the work force for the next and subsequent years
- training facilities
- staff expertise
- community contracts through pupils/students and their families
- access to certain types of funding
- status in the community
- links with higher education
- links with examining, validating bodies.

An employer might bring to a partnership:

- job opportunities

- particular (usually expensive) capital equipment
- local influence through e.g. Chamber of Commerce, Rotary, TEC etc.
- managerial expertise
- access to national fora e.g. CBI, EEF
- occasional funding for charitable/educational purposes
- work-experience placements.

There are clear 'fits' between the two lists, giving support to the view that a synergetic relationship is possible, and some obvious benefits are almost bound to derive from bringing two organisations together, just as sitting next to Nellie traditionally gradually fused the experience of the expert with the youthful vigour of the apprentice. The parallel is not exact, but it underlines the usual perception that in education/industry partnerships education tends to receive while industry tends to give. That is, I believe, an inadequate basis for a true partnership.

Part of the problem may rest in the supposed 'otherness' of the two sectors. For some years schemes have existed to encourage teachers to set out like Victorian missionaries to explore the strange and wild territory of industry and to convert its leaders to an acceptance of the virtues of education. Return visits have also been arranged. David Lodge's *Nice Work* sets this model in the context of higher education, but his conclusions about different cultures and different languages are valid for the 16-19 sector too. The trouble with these schemes is that insufficient thought was given to what they were supposed to achieve, and they inevitably perpetuated and reinforced the view of 'otherness'. At a time such as now, when vocationalism is fashionable, schools in particular but colleges also to some extent, will be characterised as not only different from industry but also inferior because of the academic or rarefied nature of much of their work. 'Real' work goes on in the 'real' world, which lies outside the gates of the school or college. This assumption needs challenge. Education is no less and no more a part of the real world than any other activity, just as mountains are as characteristic of the physical world as are plains, lakes and deserts. Those who work in schools and colleges can suffer from a sense of inadequacy or guilt which is quite absurd in its baselessness. Schools and colleges are businesses, and the Education Reform Act has confirmed this state of affairs, not created it. Their terms of trade are unusual because they have, thus far, little control of income (mostly fees) or expenditure (mostly salaries), but they sell a service to the public. When they engage in partnership activities with a company or companies the commercial aspects of their activities are often overlooked or under-rated. Similarly, companies are places of learning. If personal development is a behavioural manifestation that learning has taken place, companies are full of people experiencing learning. Much of it is unstructured and unmeasured, and in consequence overlooked and under-rated. A successful partnership should have as one of its basic principles a recognition of the similarities between participants.

It ought to be self-evident, but perhaps is not, that schools differ sharply from each other, as do colleges. These differences may derive from their size, their location, their history, their role (comprehensive, selective, opted-out, aided, special), and the personalties and priorities of their managers and governors. Some will be more businesslike, some will be better equipped, some will be growing, others in decline — all these factors directly affect both the contribution which they could make to a partnership and the objective which they would expect to gain from it. Equally wide, of course, is the variety between companies. A partnership between a large public-spirited company like Pilkington's or ICI and a school or college would not be replicated in an area in which there are no large companies at all. In a rural area the college may be the largest employer (albeit a proxy one) for miles around. A partnership between a school or college and a company on the doorstep will be different from one where the partners are separated by several miles or an extended bus journey. There can, in short, be no one model of good or successful practice. Partnerships need to be formally agreed, the details of the scheme set out as a contract managed by an executive group, and monitored as to the effectiveness. Ideally both the managing director of the company and the principal should put their names to the agreement, rather than, say, the training manager and the industrial liaison officer. It would be expected in an undertaking of this weight, that it would be endorsed by boards of directors and governors. The contract should specify all types of activity, e.g. staff exchanges; work experience; equipment loan; membership of committees; occasional lectures; holiday employment, etc, with appropriate targets and objectives for each. Such a document, like a quality assurance statement, should be designed to clarify processes and responsibilities rather than to encumber with over-elaboration. It would need to be evident that the activities were integrated into the curriculum of the school/ college, and that, for the company, the partnership was seen as essential to the planning process, like the development of a new service or product. Partnerships are not like games afternoons or general studies periods, worthy but dispensible.

Under such arrangements, work-experience might be planned thus, taking the example of a group of catering students in their first year of full-time attendance at college. The overall aims of the experience would be specified, including: to give students the opportunity to work in a real production kitchen where the pace, the expectations and the allowed tolerances would be different from a college training kitchen; to give students the chance to see and use specialist equipment unavailable at college; to give the students the opportunity to assess their own personal skills, including the ability to cope on their own, away from home. To achieve all this, and monitor it, requires detailed preparation, preferably including a presentation by the manager of the hotel in which the place of the scheme in the hotel's activities is explained, and the expectations made of students, including working hours (not necessarily the same as those of the college), lines of communication and responsibility, and details of accommodation and remuneration (free food? dormitories?). The students need to take with them to the placement properly prepared work-assignments requiring them, with the assistance of hotel staff, to observe some things, to do others and to enquire about a third group. Students might be required, for example, to sketch the layout of the kitchen, noting the position of fire-extinguishers and emergency exits, they might be asked to note the pattern of use in the restaurant; which are peak hours; what sort of music is played; what arrangements are made for smokers; what is the cleaning cycle for bedrooms and corridors; what sort of internal accounting system is used — the list could go on, but all are investigative tasks which need the help of hotel staff and which, if properly recorded can be assessed.

Alongside tests of observation, students would be required to work at different sections in the kitchen: sauce-making; larder-work; vegetable-preparation, etc. Hotel staff would be asked to note down, on customised documents, their comments on students' speed, accuracy, stamina, adaptability and demeanour, and the students themselves would contribute to their record of achievement, commenting on what they found hard, different from college, enjoyable or tedious.

Good assignments will also require the student to answer some technical catering questions and resolve syllabus issues. They will, in effect, be distance-learning materials which reinforce what the student has learned at college, locate the work-experience in its context, and indicate topics which need revision on return to the college. All this requires an enormous amount of work from both parties to the partnership, and that work represents the investment from which dividends may be expected. In the case of the catering students that dividend is a measurably better understanding of how one hotel works, and where it is effective, a thorough assignment which counts towards their final grade, and the possibility of a future job-offer. Reflection upon the experience is not only for the individual student however. It may be apparent from the head chef's comments that more time needs to be given to basic skills in the college's scheme of work or that parts of the housekeeping syllabus need revision. In the hotel it may be evident that staff could learn from the college how better to use computer-aided accountancy packages, or how to improve menu design by using desk-top publishing equipment. In the light of reading students' reports, the college might offer an updating course on health and safety regulations, or on hygiene legislation. Partnership arrangements between a college and a company or companies might encompass a range of activities, including skills-updating courses, supervisory management and intensive language tuition for example, which fall outside the scope of this chapter because they do not impact directly upon the 16-19 age group. Indirectly, of course, the fuller relationship which a whole portfolio of partnership activities offers will be likely to influence the enthusiasm with which 16–19 partnership undertakings occur. Confidence is the key to success in partnerships: the more happy experiences the better.

One example of a successful scheme which offered enhanced learning to 16–19 students and a solution to the training problems of small companies was piloted at Accrington and Rossendale College. The catering industry in East Lancashire is dominated by small hotels, a few modest-sized restaurants and some pubs with limited eating facilities. Through the college's catering Advisory Committee, membership of which is open to representatives of the industry, it was known that the catering establishments wanted training for restaurant managers in a range of topics from customer care to staff motivation. Release to college was, it was said, out of the question: they just could not be spared. A familiar impasse.

The College's offer was simply to provide students to undertake work experience — but not necessarily on a direct replacement at the same level. Arrangements were made within each catering establishment for temporary week-long promotions which, at the end of the chain, left responsibilities appropriate for full-time catering students on work-experience placement. This had the effect of providing good development opportunities to hotel and restaurant staff, excellent placements for students, the chance for restaurant managers' skills to be updated and income for the college. Four for the price of one. This model may help to resolve the problems of partnership with a number of small organisations, but it requires brokerage and quite detailed planning. This might fall to the college itself, to the local Chamber of Commerce or, more likely, to the Training and Enterprise Council (TEC). In the example given, the College's close relationship with the catering industry, covering conventional day-release, specialist courses and demonstrations, and extensive work experience dating back to the 1960s had given the mutual confidence and understanding which made an unconventional pattern worth trying. In that partnerships depend not just on technical or logistical arrangements but also personal commitment for their success they may be thought to resemble matrimony. The role of a professional matchmaker — essentially what a TEC or Chamber would do — would not be easy.

The concept of a partial partnership needs exploring. How far is it possible to speak of a partnership at all if only a restricted set of activities is undertaken? The danger of elevating the concept of partnership to an ideal relationship, laboriously defined and exclusively framed, is a real one. Perhaps it is sufficient to say that any mutually beneficial activity, properly planned, resourced and monitored is in scope, but that any member of ad hoc or unintegrated activities, however regularly they take place, are not. A partnership can, I believe, be temporary and for a fixed purpose.

An example illustrates the point.

An annual scheme brings together major employers in the engineering industry and students from schools, or more usually, colleges. The aim is to involve the students in the resolution of a genuine engineering problem, identified by the company. The students spend a given amount of time per week for a period of months, with the guidance of an assigned individual in the company and with the support of the technical staff of the school or college. At the end of the process students present their solution to a panel of mixed experts and laypeople, and answer questions about the engineering issues as well as matters to do with team-building, leadership, decision-making and planning. The main objective is to find a solution agreeable to the company in terms of its feasibility and cost. In 1990 a group of students worked with Rolls Royce at the aeroengine plant in Barnoldswick, Lancashire. The genuine problem centred on quality control in the manufacture of the honeycomb structure used inside the giant turbo blades of the current generation of engines. Faults were being discovered, but too late in the cycle to prevent significant wastage. The students devised and built a model based upon an electronic solution under computer control. It worked, it was adopted as a design worthy of further development. The scheme ended and the students had no more formal contact with Rolls Royce.

The objectives of Rolls Royce had been met — a group of highly intelligent, well-motivated students had had a good experience of the engineering industry, and their interest in an engineering career had, by their own account, been greatly increased as a result. Almost as a bonus they might have gained a very cheap solution to an expensive problem. The students' sense of achievement, heightened by the success of their carefully prepared and organised presentation, was an intended outcome fully attained. They also had access to equipment and resources not available at college. But it all worked because it was properly planned, supported and monitored. It was a self-contained project, not really suitable as the basis for other, more prolonged activities, not least because Rolls Royce and the college were too far away from each other, literally if not metaphorically. The benefits of the scheme, like the memories, will linger on. The companies involved (and they included, apart from Rolls Royce, British Nuclear Fuels and Michelin) will understand more about the nature and role of colleges and the quality and originality of the thinking displayed by the students, and all those at the college associated with the scheme, and not just the students themselves, will know, hopefully, more about the pressures, opportunities and working style of a major company. There is more to partnership than juxtaposition and faith.

Many colleges, particularly those designated as Tertiary where the relationship is closer, ordinarily describe the 11–16 high schools with which they work as 'partner' schools, rather than the unhelpfully condescending term 'feeder' schools. The emphasis is on continuity at 16+ rather than a break in the educational pattern. Colleges need to earn the trust of their partners by giving clear, unbiased advice about not only what is on offer at the college, but about the pros and cons of other options such as work or Youth Training. A college which has close relations with a variety of companies with a good record in training can point young people in the direction of these 'good' employers. In this way two kinds of partnerships overlap, like interlocking circles. This concept has been formalised in an entitlement scheme being developed in East Lancashire. The arrangements agreed and jointly administered by the Training and Enterprise Council and the local authority Careers Service, allow for the registration of over 200 companies, in the first year, which have committed themselves to offer high quality training for employees under 19. This list is carried in publicity and in information given directly to pupils in their final year of compulsory schooling. Each such pupil also receives a personalised letter reminding them of their entitlement to education and training, and guaranteeing them both an interview with an officer of the Careers Service and an offer of a place on a training scheme, in a job or in continued education. Clearly, the expectation is that young people will be steered away from companies or employers who have not undertaken to provide good quality training. Nothing in the scheme required that the training be carried out at a college — far from it — but endorsement of the scheme by local colleges is an important feature.

Nothing in the arrangements is strikingly new, except the emphasis upon an integrated pattern of post-16 opportunities. Pupils have long had the guarantee of a careers service, the promise of a YT place is familiar, and the colleges rarely turn applicants away on any ground except actual lack of room or staff, but the reminder to the young person of their rights is important, as is the willingness of large numbers of companies to take part in what amounts to a joint recruitment exercise. The scheme reinforces the links between colleges and companies, and underlines the obvious point that the differences between full-time education including planned work experience, a training place which combines work-based learning with off-the-job training and education, and a job which guarantees access to further education are ones of shading and emphasis, not kind. All three experiences lead, by a slightly different route, to similar qualifications. No unwise promise is made that the young person can choose freely from the range of possibilities — only that an 'appropriate' opportunity will be offered. The incentives to seek and follow advice, to think long-term rather than short, and to work for the best results at 16+ are all clearly set out. This sort of scheme will be even more effective when credit transfer arrangements are in place, when the vocational and academic routes are intertwined, and when issues of perceived different status as between tracks are resolved. The essentials of a partnership are present from the start: the process is carefully planned, outcomes are clear, ownership is shared, and a coherent set of available quality measures exists.

This scheme has similarities with Compacts, which concentrate however, mostly on the pre-16 phase, and with the various pilots for post-16 vouchers, and the simplicity and accessibility of the scheme make it particularly attractive.

The Education Reform Act required college governing bodies to be dominated by employer interests, and it is normally a requirement that at least 50% of the attendance at any governing body meeting should be from the employer sector. This is an opportunity to strengthen existing partnerships by securing board membership from a linked company, or to begin the process of negotiation which might lead to a productive partnership where none exists thus far. It would be helpful if some reciprocal arrangement led to college representation on the board of an appropriate company. Probably the most effective direct influence by employment interests on the college curriculum comes from their membership of course committees. A BTEC Business and Finance Course committee which included a well-briefed bank manager, company accountant or finance director would be able to devise assignments which reflected or drew upon genuine business examples. Many such course committees also include students, and the process of design, construction, review, modification and report models an industrial or commercial product cycle very illuminatingly. The essence is shared responsibility for success or failure, measured by the increasingly familiar yardsticks of enrolments as compared with targets, retention rates, results of assessment and examination, and costs per successful student. These indicators, *mutatis mutandis*, are commercial/industrial ones. An employer feels at ease with the application of these standards to the education process, and can advise on the methodology. An employer from a partnership company should consider membership of a course committee as a right rather than a favour, and the college should see the invitation as an obligation not a dispensation. Such arrangements are not uncommon, but the reverse is very rare.

There is no good reason why so few educationalists sit on company boards. College staff often contribute to the management of local enterprise agencies, to small business clubs and sit on the committees of Chambers of Commerce. They also, in a different pattern, are active in Rotary Clubs and similar organisations. Yet their close knowledge of the local community, their personal experience of curriculum innovation with a far-reaching impact like TVEI or the National Curriculum, and, in many cases, their role in the training of company employees on release to college are not usually exploited by companies. Such neglect undermines what should be the mutuality of a partnership. It is possible that those who work in education, even at senior management level, lack the confidence to press for this sort of recognition; a diffidence which has its origin in the perceived 'otherness' referred to above, combined with the erroneous view that education has little or nothing to offer a commercial boardroom. In fact there are no no-go areas for education.

Towns which are twinned with equivalents in other countries

announced the fact as you enter. They do so proudly rather than furtively, reckoning that the partnership is of self-evident benefit. Why do not schools or colleges display at their gate or on their notepaper or in their prospectus 'Twinned with Philips' or 'Partnered with Boots'? And why do not companies return the compliment at their gate? The many levels and manifestations of town twinning, as developed by the twinning committee, have much in common with the variety and range of activities which might be shared between a college or school and a company, as developed by the partnership committee.

The vitality of a partnership will depend not only upon its perceived value but on its variety, and ideally it might involve both students and staff in different activities. One example draws upon lecturing staff technical skills. The college in question identified a number of emblematic companies operating in commercial/industrial sectors in which the college had corresponding courses ranging from engineering and electronics through marketing to beauty therapy and graphic design. Each of these companies was invited to accept a field officer, a college lecturer with a half-day per week freed up from teaching for the purpose. The role of the lecturer was to act as a channel of communication between company and college, to explain each to the other, to organise and perhaps deliver bespoke short courses, and to contribute his or her skills to the company. An electronics lecturer, for example, assisted the company with the development of a product, and a motor vehicle lecturer spent time in the repair shop. The benefits for 16-19 year students are self evident: the lecturer's knowledge of the trade or industry is bang up-to-date, many students secured good work-experience in the partner companies, and the overall reputation of the college was enhanced. Such arrangements are not easy to achieve, not all field officers managed to deploy their technical expertise while at the company, and some firms were cautious about commercial confidentiality. But where it worked, it worked very well, not least because of the logic of the exchange: companies release staff to give occasional, specialist lectures, the college releases staff to give an occasional, specialist contribution to the production or service process.

What can go wrong with partnerships between colleges and industry? Staleness can set in, so that one partner or both cease to be inventive, settle for the familiar and thus fail to move the partnership along. When this happens, better or more useful alternatives are missed, perhaps with new companies or new colleges. A programme of activities which has not changed for, say two years may need review and amendment. Cosiness can be stultifying. A partnership which depends upon personal contacts or friendships between individuals can collapse when they move on to another job, and this would be a sign that the partnership was not properly 'owned' by the institutions concerned. A firm or college can change its culture quite markedly if the chief executive of either is replaced, and new priorities or new perspectives could kill off a partnership very rapidly. A series of bad experiences, such as ill-disciplined students or an insensitive works-manager will jeopardise a partnership, as will differing practices on, for example, equal opportunities. Such casualties are from time to time inevitable, and argue for a set of partnerships rather than just one. A good college will have a target replacement rate for obsolescent courses, and it will also plan to renegotiate a pattern of partnerships at an agreed tempo. Stagnation is the first stage of decay. Inappropriate expectations made of partnerships can be equally lethal: a college calculating that extensive work-experience will overcome staff shortages in crucial curriculum areas, for example, or a company looking to use unpaid students to help in the production process at times of peak demand. Each organisation is distinct, but, as has been outlined above, has spheres of overlapping interest. It is within these overlaps that partnerships flourish, outside of them lurk problems of exploitation, resentment and the breakdown of a relationship.

Chapter 7: Partnership: one school's experience

Graham Elliott

The school context

Hinde House School is located in the North-East of Sheffield with a catchment area which is adjacent to the M1 overlooking the Tinsley Viaduct. During the 1980s both the community and its schools suffered from the severe effects of deindustrialisation, which for the schools was compounded by an above average drop in pupil numbers caused by a fall in the birth rate. Whilst the planned regeneration of this part of the city, including the Meadowhall retail development, has brought hope of an economic recovery, the area is still coping with the effects of unemployment and reduced school budgets.

In the last five years there has been a clear commitment from the Nursery/First, Middle and Comprehensive schools to work in a co-operative and supportive way, resulting in a pyramid of schools developing coherence and continuity for young people in the area from the ages 3–16. The ensuing provision of curriculum and transition strategies by these schools has brought confidence in and quality to the educational provision within the statutory age range.

The introduction of a Tertiary College system in 1987 meant that Hinde House School became a 12–16 age range comprehensive school which by 1990 had a roll of 620. This change also made imperative the development of links with employers, Youth Training providers and the tertiary colleges so that the quality of transition for young people was as effective into the post-16 area as it had been throughout their school career.

The 'Great Debate' about education had been underway for

some time and though it was clear that the curriculum was in need of change, it was less clear how much change should take place at Hinde House, bearing in mind the need for teachers to have ownership of curriculum delivery if higher standards and a wide range of learning experiences were to permeate the whole curriculum rather than making a series of peripheral and ephemeral alterations to an already redundant approach.

Hinde House was a fairly typical school in that there had been a recognition of the need to relate to the 'World of Work', 'Employers', 'Further and Higher Education', 'Preparation for Adult Life' and many of the other banner headings which at different times were placed before us by non-school organisations.

The measurable effect of this concern and the response to it was, to be honest, very limited. In year groups of 200 students some 10–30 might undertake a work-experience with little preparation, follow-up or curriculum related activity. There was a twinning arrangement with a local employer which involved one member of staff and a limited number of students. This contact was increasingly in danger of disappearing due to the economic pressures on the company, and, by the same token, budget pressures on the school which were making it difficult to commit teacher time to a non-class contact time activity.

Into this situation came the decision of Sheffield Eduction Department to provide support for curriculum development in secondary schools by providing cover for the release of five teachers to undertake school focused curriculum development in the academic year 1986-7. At Hinde House this team of teachers was selected by the staff and centred its attention on the transition from middle schools to the secondary sector and the curriculum which should be provided in the Y8 group. In successive years further secondments though reduced in number, were available, and these provided a pool of resource which schools could direct towards the review, development, implementation and evaluation of curriculum change. As will be seen later, access to this kind of resource was to be a powerful influence in developing a partnership and its activities.

Need for development

When the idea of a school-industry partnership was first mooted a fundamental question required answering before time and resource could be committed to its development. Given the number of curriculum tasks which the school needed to address and the limited resources available to make a response with, the case had to be made not only for a partnership itself, but also for the prioritisation of this task over other needs which had been identified.

At Hinde House we were aware of the changes inherent in taking all the proposals, concerns and issues in education, attempting a series of separate and discreet changes, and then finding a lack of coherence regarding the whole curriculum, with the added possibility of incomplete and ineffective curriculum change causing frustration amongst teaching staff.

It did seem, however, that a series of needs which were surfacing could be responded to and change enhanced through the creation of an industry/school partnership.

● Whatever the changes in terms of content and process of the curriculum the quality of student experience could be enhanced by the exposure of the whole curriculum to the 'real' world. The developments proposed by our staff secondees and the introduction of GCSE both promoted the need for practical and relevant applications of learning experiences in the context of the world beyond school.

● Most schools reorganised their governing bodies in Autumn 1988. Hinde House was no exception and the outgoing governing body wished to recommend co-opted governors who would have a commitment to and involvement with the school. Partners would be ideally suited for this role, and with the local management of schools becoming imminent, would provide much needed skills and expertise.

● The school was hoping to be part of the Sheffield TVEI extension programme. Within the Sheffield proposal and Training Agency requirements, a high profile was given to the development of Careers Education and Guidance, Work-Experience, industry visits and work shadowing, all of which could be provided through a partnership.

● The school had a guidance programme which needed to develop a range of activities and contacts with employees, trainers and further education institutions so that students could make career choices in an informed and knowledgeable way.

● Many of the needs described above require the involvement of a school staff who have an understanding of and commitment to the benefits of linking with the world beyond school. The introduction of a partnership would provide the opportunity for developing a staff/industry interface.

● It would be easy for the issues to be addressed by a series of discrete activities undertaken by different staff with the likelihood of overlap, empire building, and gate-keeping. It became clear that the effectiveness of our work in the industry area would require the involvement of many staff, through an integrated approach to our school-industry relationship. With hindsight this final point should have been given more significance from the start. It is however, difficult to perceive the potential benefits to industrial partners in advance of an activity.

At the back of our minds however, was a feeling that partnership could provide the school with an opportunity for working within our community to develop inter-industry contact which could be beneficial for all concerned.

There were probably other factors at work, which have since slipped automatically into place, but the needs expressed above were evident, being expressed by a range of people, and provided a justification for investing time and resource in trying to establish a partnership with industry. It had become clear that this also needed to be educational activity, with a high profile for curriculum and the quality of student experiences, with any material gain for the school being a bonus rather than *raison d'etre*.

This was an important first principle, and one which we constantly have to remind ourselves of in days of limited resources. As a school we did not want to be seen as constantly rolling out the begging bowl. Our aim was to be an equal partner in enhancing student experiences.

Methodology

The school's identification of needs was slowly emerging through the environment which prevailed in the educational world during the last half of the 1980s. How to respond to such needs was a different matter entirely. There had been severe de-industrialisation for a decade within the local economy with substantial and permanent job losses, particularly in steel and engineering. Within Sheffield there was much discussion about economic recovery and social development requiring the efforts and energies of all members of the community. In January 1988 a signed partnership between Education and the Business community called the Sheffield Contract was brought into existence.

This high profile contract included the establishment of the Sheffield Education Business Partnership with a brief to encourage the setting up of a programme of coherent Education/Business links across the curriculum of schools and colleges.

The approach used by Sheffield was particularly helpful, in

that it established credibility for partnership at the highest level, with a supportive framework for development. Hinde House was one of ten comprehensive schools approached in the first year with a view to the launching of a school/industry partnership. As far as our school was concerned the timing of this initiative was a perfect match with our stage of development. If this had not been the case, we would have had serious reservations about participation. In our view one of the difficulties associated with curriculum initiatives which originate from outside of the school is the temptation to say yes to good ideas, funds, and other resources,when the school has not reached the point where this particular initiative fits into its evolutionary development of staff and curriculum. Effective school management uses external initiatives as a prompt to and support for the logical next stage of a school's development.

Having agreed to our participation in the formation of school/industry partnership (both school management and Governors were enthusiastic), we proceeded with central support to plan a launch conference for May 1988. We followed the programme devised centrally, which proved to be a bonus when companies wishing to link into more than one school could identify readily what was happening as the process was common to each school.

The launch conference was successful in many ways, one of which was the opportunity it gave for students and staff to display the already high quality of work across many areas of the curriculum. A full report was published to all who attended and from this 11 employers expressed a willingness to attend further meetings and become involved actively in an education business partnership with Hinde House School.

At this point the school had to make a decision about the priority which this activity was to be given in the school's development. Did we envisage the development of partnership as an additional responsibility for the staff involved? Could non-contact time be found? Was its success depend on a proper investment of resources by the school?

The school had the equivalent of two full-time secondments available through the Sheffield school focused development programme. Having carefully considered all the alternatives it was decided that our staff would be invited to apply for one secondment to explore the area of school industry links, with an emphasis on the development of a partnership. The flexibility of the school focused secondment programme was fully demonstrated during the following year, when the secondee was able to develop a new programme for work experience (with

Partnership involvement) and explore the feasibility of Compact, again with a full contribution from the partnership.

It is interesting that the Governors in their 1991–92 budget have created a sum of money for staff release of the secondment type, in anticipation of the curriculum planning required in school as the Local Education Authority proposal to change the age of transfer from 12+ to 11+ is expected to materialise September 1992.

This was of course a whole curriculum, whole staff development, and the secondee needed access to the staff in a structured and formal way rather than being reliant on informal and ad hoc contacts. This meant that our annual plan for the curriculum training days needed to recognise and reflect the training needs arising from the secondee's work. Curriculum days were allocated for training and followed later by in-service specifically aimed at form tutors of the relevant year groups.

These developments and the support provided for them were constantly underpinned by the continued demonstration of commitment to partnership by the school's Governors and senior management team.

The outcome of this approach has been a high profile for Partnership and its associated activities, which has given confidence and a feeling of success to the teaching staff and partners who have felt able to undertake a wide range of activities. From a school management point of view, valuable lessons about the nature of curriculum change, the processes involved and the need to plan for and provide adequate time and resource for all staff involved, have been learnt. This, as described earlier has helped the Governors recognise with clarity the need to invest in non-contact time for teachers and appropriate training for all staff when change is envisaged, if the proposed development is to be absorbed fully into the ethos and curriculum of the school.

Achievements

The continued existence of an activity which is totally voluntary for all involved must hinge on the real outcomes being perceived by those participating as being of sufficient value for their continued involvement to be worthwhile. To some extent partnership was a new concept, asking industry to make an on-going commitment to an activity which had no previous examples which would recommend it. Indeed for a number of meetings there was an exchange of views about education, training and industry and increasing concern about whether partnership added anything to previous links, replaced them, or was simply another talking shop. At that time many of us did not fully appreciate the merit of exploring shared values and issues, largely I suspect because there was an absence of a specific and measurable goal which we could work towards.

Fortunately, the work of our secondee was directly relevant in producing an approach for introducing a three week work experience for all our Year 11 pupils. The Partnership accepted the task as a priority for the school and helped develop and deliver a programme which ensured that all students received thorough preparation, had an appropriate placement, and participated in a thorough de-briefing, thus providing a QUALITY work experience. The use of the phrase 'quality experience' has now become synonomous with the school's industry partnership.

The identifiable success of this activity, which included use of partners' premises for staff training, and the direct involvement of partners with both students and staff, resulted in a clearer view of the partnership's potential in curriculum terms. This led the partners towards a request that the school produce a plan for its Guidance programme from which the partners could identify and prioritise the support which they could offer towards enhancing our activities and adding to the quality of our provision. This request was important in that it forced the staff involved in Guidance to review the programme and look at the students' experiences in totality. In fact this exercise was undertaken for the whole school, and led to a number of improvements to the programme in all year groups.

The practical target was the provision of three planned visits to places of work for all students in Year 10 during the summer term. Our partners found other willing companies, helped plan the programme and on its completion were able to assist in tackling the logistics problems which occur with such an exercise.

The launch of Compact also provided a focus for debate about business and education links and the partners here made a major contribution to our thinking, delivery and evolution of a COMPACT scheme.

The existence of a partnership has also provided an appropriate forum through which external agencies can be channelled. The ideas proposed by the Sheffield Education Business Partnership and services such as the Teacher Placement Service can be given an appropriate context within the partnership. For example, through the Teacher Placement Service the Head undertook a three week placement at Boots PLC in Meadowhall, fulfilling one of the agreed aims, which was to recruit a retail partner, as this sizeable area of employment was not represented within the partnership.

Individual partners have contributed in many ways, stressing the point that the school can identify and seek response to needs within a clearly agreed framework. There are four partners who are school governors, providing not only their skills and expertise, but a real understanding of the school through practical involvement. Numerous visits both to the school and out to the partners are taking place across the whole curriculum. One partner provides a school bank run by pupils, whilst others have provided projects for curricular activity.

The whole of the school community feels positive about the involvement of partners and the activities which have been introduced or enhanced through their existence. These achievements stem from the core aims which link with school values, concern for quality in education, and the merit of the 'partnership' notion, providing a framework for activity.

All of this, and no mention of money or material resources!! Our partnership has never been aimed at a resourcing of the school in a material sense, but has focused on the educational experiences of students and their provision at the highest quality possible. Many of our partners work in industries where finance and resources are as hard to come by as they are in education. This does not mean that such support is not available or forthcoming for genuine development. Our work-experiences booklet is sponsored, materials for Technology and improvement of the school's environment have been supplied. Sponsorship of an Arts Week and Events Week enabled both to take place, and the donation of physical resources is gratefully received. Much of this support is on a self-help basis. For example, one partner facilitated the removal of carpet tiles so that our staff and parents have been able to carpet most of the school.

The future

As the partnership evolves and grows there is a need for an ongoing review of its activities linked with new issues facing the school. In the same year that the school seconded a member of staff to develop the school-industry relationship, our second secondment was in many ways closely related in that we released a member of staff with a brief about the development of a Record of Achievement and Experience (RAE). This commenced with the Year eight pupils and for the first time in 1991, we will be presenting all our school leavers with a RAE which again we feel will be of a high quality. In forming a school validation board for RAE and Compact, members of the partnership will be able to join a group of parents and staff and make a valuable contribution in their own right, and also as people who are knowledgeable about the school.

As serious partnership activities are put into practice, there is a growing need for an annual programme and audit of activity, so that the quality of experience offered to students each year is maintained as planning and organisations are renewed.

From its inception, the Partnership has encouraged the involvement of students in its discussions and decisions. This is never an easy matter and the mere attendance of students at a meeting can create the impression of real involvement when this is a long way from reality. Within school the Compact development has involved the introduction of target setting and action planning by and for individual students. This has been used as an agenda item by the partnership, through which student participation has been encouraged as indeed the pupil setting and review of progress within the RAE provides further stimulus to effective student involvement.

Other scenarios come to mind when exploring further areas of development for the partnership. The use of effective co-operation between industry and education is not limited to the secondary sector, and many primary schools are introducing existing curriculum activity for their pupils by working closely with industry. Within our own catchment area considerable progress has been made towards developing the concept of a pyramid of schools working together to create coherence and continuity in curriculum and effective transition from school to school throughout the 3–16 age range. The industry partnership is now exploring ways in which it can serve the pyramid schools as a whole rather than focus simply on the secondary stage.

There are also recognised areas of common interest which we have still to explore. There are joint needs in terms of personal and management development for staff, for example, in exploring the issues and practices connected with training, staff appraisal, and recruitment methods.

Conclusions

The investment of time and resources in any activity requires the provision of clear aims, practical implementation, and monitored outcomes. The justification for an involvement in partnership can readily be found on philosophical grounds about which there is little dispute. Converting theory into practice is much more difficult and some of the issues involved at this stage are worthy of consideration.

● The initial and on-going commitment by the school's Governors and management team, demonstrated by the provision of resources and an organisational framework which facilitates and encourages activity is an essential feature in the establishment of a partnership.
● Many of the activities undertaken by the partnership can be provided by a school without using this form of organisation. The justification of the partnership approach is that it encourages the notions of quality and excellence, whilst providing a framework within which a wide range of activities can be given a sense of coherence and wholeness.
● By establishing a partnership it is likely that the school must recognise its own role in servicing, supporting, and maintaining the progress of its partnership, in the same way that it would for any internal group.
● Partners will feel commitment and involvement if clear and agreed frameworks for activity are defined and there is task orientation with measurable outcomes. It is not viable to create agenda items which partners will find irrelevant or unmanageable.
● Partners will vary in their ability and willingness to commit time to partnership activities. This may help to explain the difficulty faced in involving small businesses in partnership activities. An environment must be created in which partners can feel free to raise or lower their involvement as is appropriate. Partnership should not be competitive but supportive to all involved.
● Many partners make personal commitments to a school, for others they are representing their companies' commitment to this activity, and for some it is their job. Over a period of time the effects of changes in personal circumstances and company policy mean that a viable partnership will need to recruit new partners and plan for effective induction.

Above all, Partnership has added an exciting and stimulating impetus to the development of our school. It has helped industry see the quality of provision and feel a genuine responsibility for and involvement in making high quality educational experiences available to our students; in promoting excellence. For our part, we have learnt a considerable amount about the world beyond school, made many friends, and seen our school and its curriculum develop in a positive healthy way.

Chapter 8: Partnership in a development project: The Teacher Placement Service

Peter Davies and Bill Fisher

Introduction

This chapter provides an opportunity for us to state clearly the role and importance of the Teacher Placement Service (TPS), our success and potential role within partnerships. The practice of providing secondments to education and business is unique in education business liaison because it requires participants to transcend the barriers of classroom or workplace to break out of their normal work pattern behaviour and to learn by direct experience from others' work settings. In these few words we may only point to the kaleidoscope of enthusiasm and activity by secondess that has been generated across the country in such a short space of time.

The Teacher Placement Service (TPS) is partnership in-service. Its model of operation may be of interest to readers participating in the management of partnership activities in general. Firstly, its operating principles and structures are unparalleled in education business liaison. Through the work of the teacher placement organisers available in each authority together with a national support service, there exists a combination of a devolved, flexible and supportive structure focused on a strategic national frame-work of aims and objectives. Secondly, it has been successful both in terms of increasing its obvious and immediate performance locally and nationally, and also in terms of preparing people for a wider involvement in partnership development in new and less obvious directions. Thirdly, there is its distinctive role within existing as well as emerging partnership activity and the contribution made as a foundation for all future developments within these partnerships.

Teacher Placement Service will be a key activity of Education-Business Partnerships, representing the basic building block of partnership activity. It is vital that such activity is based on recent and relevant experience of the business and education environment which builds mutual confidence. Placements provide a simple yet powerful mechanism for developing understanding and stimulating change through addressing the heart of the cultural divide. The quality and relevance of pupil work experience, curriculum development, careers education and guidance and other key partnership areas will be dependent on a teaching profession with a positive attitude to the role of business based on first hand experience.

> Teachers' understanding of industry will influence their attitudes towards it, and the attitudes of their students. This understanding needs to be informed, up-to-date and backed by first-hand experience, not based on hearsay or second-hand impressions.[1]
>
> *Partnership: Working with Education:* DES, 1987.

The significance of this in terms of teacher learning is the way in which teacher placement supports a broad based professional development model which integrates with specific and general school issues and is attractive because it is beyond the conventional forms of in-service providing a radical, memorable experience in a teacher's career.

The provision of secondments to business and education is not a new concept. For many years secondment has been a local activity of variable quality and quantity. Very rarely has such experience been shared amongst a wider group of community partners. The arrival of the TPS nationally has made the difference not only to the quantity of this activity, but in significant qualitative and strategic ways. We would argue that far from being just another fashionable initiative it should be seen as a strategy for delivering significant partnership objectives. This provides the service with a unique operational advantage to appraise partnerships in action.

Background

The 1988 White Paper. (DTI)[2]
The Department for Enterprise set out an initiative to encourage the growth of links between schools and the world of work. The

key element of this enterprise and education initiative was the specific target that, 'Each year 10% of teachers should have the opportunity to gain personal experience in the world of business'.

The Department of Trade and Industry recognised the effectiveness of teacher placements in promoting a working partnership between education and industry by identifying the placement programme as a central element of the initiative. Following the publication of the White Paper, *Understanding British Industry (UBI)* was contracted to the Department of Trade and Industry in order to set up, monitor and evaluate a series of pilot programmes. The report on this work *Teacher Placement Programme 1988*[3] was presented to the DTI in December 1988 and provided the basis for the setting up of the Teacher Placement Service in April 1989.

Teacher placement in industry have formed the backbone of the UBI activities since the project was set up in 1977, but formal schemes date back to the early 1960s, with LEAs such as Leicestershire acting as pioneers in the field when the Confederation of British Industry (CBI) first piloted the three week *Introduction to Industry Scheme* for teachers. The development of these schemes was based on:

1. The need to close the traditional cultural divide between education and industry where 'many entered the teaching profession straight from Higher Education without much practical knowledge of conditions in industry, or a proper understanding of its role and requirements'.[4]
2. The effect of the 'multiplier principle' of the influence of a teacher on innumerable pupils. What was taught was often exclusively decided by the teacher. The preliminary step to any change of educational practice as to how pupils are introduced to and learn about industry should involve direct experience and regular industrial updating for teachers.

The first point is supported by the DES Survey[5] and the CBI Task Force[6] which suggested that approximately 90% of the current teaching force have:

> no direct experience of working in industry (outside vacation experience)

and that:

> many generations of pupils will gain from teacher experience of industry.   *Industry Matters.*

The growth of the schools/industry movement and the advent of new organisations such as UBI and SCIP (School Curriculum Industry Partnership) in the late 1970s provided the real stimulus for the development of the teacher placement schemes, which were now geared more towards the positive use of industrial experience in the educational process, and accepted as being part of the further professional development of a teacher. This shift in focus was further supported by educational initiatives such as TVEI and GCSE, which demanded greater relevance and allowed for the integration of teacher placement courses into the in-service training provision.

The Teacher Placement Service 1989–91

The present Teacher Placement Service structure became operational during 1989 and began to translate its bold target of 10% of teachers receiving industrial placements each year into a reality.

Throughout these early days the service was faced with problems of misinterpretation about its purpose amongst the educational community. Messages were transmitted that this was to be work experience for teachers. The headline, 'Factory Holidays For Teachers' confirmed the worst. Views were expressed: 'Not only do we need to experience real work,' went the argument, 'but we should give up our holiday times to do it!' The proposal was evidently servicing a deficit model of education, which diagnosed that something was wrong with teachers which industry could put right: this at a time when education was faced by changes of revolutionary proportions, new content through curriculum reform required by the Education Reform Act and GCSE, new models of learning, new forms of assessment e.g. Records of Achievement; new organisations e.g. tertiary colleges; new accountability, newly appointed parent and industrial governors, new professionalism through initial teacher education, and training reforms for employment training. It seemed feasible to some in the profession that, in releasing pressurised teachers to enjoy the experience of a different context, they might choose never to return. The reverse has proved to be the case. Teachers reaffirm their commitment to their pupils and schools.

The four principles

The Teacher Placement Service is founded on four basic principles:

1) Partnership
2) Quality
3) Ownership
4) Integration.

1. *Partnership* here includes:
   (i) that between employers, host organisations and educational authorities in the delivery of this service;
   (ii) the return placement from business into schools. Reciprocal placements by industry into schools is important both in terms of the quality and purpose that TPS brings to partnership activity.

Host organisations of the service (LEAs, Chambers of Commerce, Local Employer Organisations) were the recipients of grants based on £5 per teacher for the area and were responsible for the local delivery of the service. In each case a working relationship had to be established between employment and education sectors, not without difficulty in certain areas where a lack of trust and respect between potential partners served only to highlight the depth of the cultural divide.

2. *Quality* here includes:
   (i) quality of experience for the employer and teacher on placement through careful preparation and follow-up;
   (ii) quality of service offered at local, regional and national level;
   (iii) quality of change in the education system as a result of placement programmes.

Quality in teacher placements might be measured in terms of the formation of a partnership between school and industry that effects change in the classroom for the benefit of the pupil. In this sense, the placement in industry will not be viewed as an end in itself but as an essential ingredient in the process of change with the quality of the outcome being dependent on the design and management of the whole process. Quality as we have stated is the basis for growth. The quality of the service provided is dependent on the key elements of the placement process.

It is the quality of each individual experience which is vital to the Teacher Placement Service and how organisers do everything to ensure that the preparation, matching and follow up support is of the highest standard. Evaluation returns from the 1990 cohort (2,966) shows that 96 % of teachers and 93 % of companies reported that briefings successfully prepared them for a placement, while 89% of teachers successfully met their placement objectives. This finding is very encouraging, but the real benefits are only evident from the activities generated following placement. The expanding national collection of case studies highlights the variety of outcomes at all levels and in particular features examples of placements for industrialists in education organised as part of the service. Equally a wide range of quality materials has been introduced to support industrial placements.

3. *Ownership* here includes:
    (i) that of the TPS at the local level, ideally with the school in partnership with its local economic community;
    (ii) that of placements by the local community (as distinct from DTI or UBI).

The Teacher Placement Service was a DTI initiative but the service needed to encourage local ownership and, therefore, needed to be flexible in its approach to each of the teacher placement organisers working in any particular area.

Each organiser therefore is responsible for the production of a local development plan, which sets out the strategy for meeting the targets. This development plan is prepared in negotiation with the education and business partnership and must be agreed on by the TPS regional manager. The development plan therefore should contain partnership goals and reflect the local priorities, as well as include key programme goals of the service.

4. *Integration* here includes:
    (i) that of the TPS into the staff and curriculum development policies of the education authorities and schools;
    (ii) into the training plans for the delivery of educational initiative - National Curriculum, TVEI, etc;
    (iii) into the education liaison policies of companies.

Education traditionally has taught, trained and certificated its own through in-house courses and Higher Education institutions and teachers' routes to personal and professional development have remained within the educational sphere. There is much to be learnt from recognising demands within industry and working on them. Physically and psychologically crossing the boundary into a different culture has provided a wide range of learning experiences for teachers. It is important to emphasise that the impact of the Teacher Placement Service is far greater than the sum of teachers taking placement, as evaluative returns and case study evidence consistently point to the experience as a stimulus for change and the development of partnership activities. One issue is how the experience maybe evaluated over the short and long term. Designing the placement programme is a question of understanding the process which is operating and the effect this is having as the experience proceeds. Many education and business strategies never achieve significant change through their service to partnership; at best they are effective support work, at worst they are irrelevant.

It is important for the organiser to assist teachers to prepare specific objectives for placement. Experience tells us that teachers with specific objectives rather than the general 'to find out about industry' have the most successful placements. Indeed where objectives are negotiated and agreed in collaboration with school or department colleagues, then there is usually more support and subsequent action following placements.

The experience can be a vehicle for delivering related curriculum objectives such as the preparation of course work. Management development opportunities through shadowing managerial roles and processes provide a contrast and comparison for reflection on the management of education. In this respect, the organiser continues to integrate the experience into schools and local authority plans, rather than perceiving it as an additional bolt-on training opportunity.

Teacher placement organisers

The role of the organiser is vital in providing careful preparation and support so as to ensure that identifiable outcomes result from the placement. The process of effectively managed placements in business must be to encourage the development of a partnership which effects change in the classroom for the benefit of the pupil. The most important ingredient for the effectiveness of industrial placements for teachers and business is the design of the briefing and debriefing process. Schemes which place teachers into industry without adequate preparation or follow up usually offer little of lasting value and may even have a detrimental effect on the relationship between education and industry.

The Teacher Placement Service now has 131 teacher placement organisers and covers every local education authority in England, Wales and Scotland. Within a time span of two years has emerged an extensive network of education business practitioners using a variety of backgrounds and experiences in a variety of operating conditions.

The national service

It may appear contradictory, at a time when so much emphasis is given to restructuring business/education liaison around the notion of local solutions to local problems, for the Teacher Placement Service to retain a national project team comprising project director and regional managers. The project team's stated role is to ensure the effective delivery of the TPS within each region and to continue to increase the volume of high quality teacher placements in business and, simultaneously, encourage greater involvement of business people in schools. The network of regional managers are UBI's primary link with the organisers on an individual basis, facilitating:

● The monitoring and processing of contracts with host organisations.
● The support and development for the organiser service within the region.

In reality, the role of the project team and its contribution has been much more expansive. The regional managers occupy a crucial role in providing a strategic framework for management of the Teacher Placement Service. They have been required to:

● provide training, induction programmes, specific group events based on the training needs of organisers
● encourage the development of a network which incorporates other education liaison groups and activities
● disseminate good practice within the region and through the national network
● organise national initiatives e.g. Open University Accreditation
● develop business initiatives with headquarter companies which attract private sponsorship into the service
● work on a national focus to encourage support from other government departments and national institutions
● co-ordinate national advertising and publicity campaigns
● collect and present statistical returns on all aspects of the national service
● offer advice and consultation at national and local levels on

policy and practice in the provision of in-service for teachers under Grants for Educational Support and Training (GEST)[7].

The TPS has worked with the School Management Task Force to ensure that placements form an integral element in the career profile of teachers. A series of regional seminars were held with the consortia identified by the School Management Task Force.

The National Curriculum Council has jointly produced a poster and publications entitled *Secondments Into Industry* which have been distributed widely into all staff rooms in the country.

A closer partnership between schools and industry is needed in the implementation of the broad National Curriculum. It cannot and must not be confined to the school and to the classroom. There will have to be fuller use even than now of the invaluable expertise and experience of the community and that means largely the business and industrial community... The National Curriculum gives through design and technology, maths, science and subjects yet to come the potential for developing practical skills as never before. Schools cannot achieve a major change on this and the 'basics' unaided by the rest of us. The Teacher Placement Service has a key role as any in this.[8]

Duncan G. Graham, CBE, MA, Chairman and Chief Executive, National Curriculum Council.

Reviewing performance

Over the operational period the Teacher Placement Service has increased the levels of activity from an estimated 1,900 teachers into industry in 1989 to in excess of 20,000 in the first two years. The importance of statistical returns is a much debated issue with individual organisers. At the local level it may not always be easy to equate a framework of locally agreed targets with the specific levels of achievement nationally. It is such measurable levels of activity over a given time period however which provide a means of support and comparison.

An immediate response might be that quantity appears to be all that counts. However, it is these measurable indicators which distinguish the service from many other education business strategies. Too often in the past, schools/industry work has suffered from an inability to present value for money indicators and this we suggest is one of the strengths of the TPS. Statistical returns have played a vital role in the ability to present the activities of the service, nationally and locally in a simple understandable format. Indeed the ability to produce a range of returns on value for money indices has been a major factor in securing continued treasury funding.

Teacher Placement Service as a foundation of education business partnerships

Teacher placement is a basic building block for partnership. The activity is straightforward, understandable, accessible and develops the mutual confidence and understanding on which other partnership activities can be built.

The organiser contribution is to offer an experience which may illuminate the lack of understanding of other organisations and promotes the development of effective partnership. Placement may assist in pulling together the framework and coherent objectives for partnerships; can explore how other organisations may be used; is able to secure commitment to growth by partners through direct experience of one another; establishes communications between the various partners; may be used to identify who should be involved and at what levels; provides a regular data and information flow through its exchange mechanism; may indicate for the local area the support available from national employers that may be utilised at the local level; constructs environments where introductions are purposeful between the partners and can adopt an incremental approach to partnership activity.

The Department of Employment in their *Partnership Handbook* publication[9], recommend and increase in the numbers of teachers undertaking secondment into industry as a key performance indicator of partnership activity, as it has been of the TVEI extension programme.

The service has raised difficult questions and made fundamental demands on these partnerships in the effort to achieve the national goals of the service. The merits of these coalitions are that through direct discussions and active support they should raise as many questions as they pose. They are not comfortable structures where representatives discuss the virtues of any activity. They require movement, things to happen — a creative tension. The issues discussed should make demands on members, require understanding, discussion of the panacea, introduce, inform, involve.

Working partnerships are symbolised through the culture of

their practitioners and their patterns of interaction on a daily basis: teams working within teams focused through national, regional, down to local level. Effective integration and team building by education business members can be helped or hindered by the significance that partnerships apply to this process.

Case study of the Teacher Placement Service role within a local business education partnership

The experience of Mid Glamorgan highlights the practical aspects of the service operating as a member of a partnership team.

The Mid Glamorgan Education Business Partnership has been in operation since 1989. Its mission is to establish effective links between education and business. Its steering group consists of very senior figures from education and business. Over 150 businesses support the work of partnership. The partnership consists of seconded educationalists and business people who are responsible for a number of different programmes ranging from enterprise to joint management training. Since its inception a major programme has been teacher placements with the partnership becoming host to the teacher placement organiser for Mid Glamorgan.

The teacher placement organiser has a varied role within the partnership. As well as the traditional role of arranging for teachers to spend time in business other responsibilities have been assumed by the teacher placement organiser. These include being responsible for publicity and the marketing of the partnership. In addition the teacher placement organiser is seen as part of the partnership 'team' and therefore expected to become involved in partnership activities as and when required. This has resulted in the teacher placement organiser being able to influence both the day to day running and longer term decision making of partnership.

At first glance it may seem that the TPS in Mid Glamorgan has become diluted as more and more time is spent on other partnership activities. This has certainly not been the case. In return for the teacher placement organiser's involvement there is full support from the rest of the partnership team.

This has a number of benefits:

• A team of nine is far more effective than a single person in making contact with schools. There are almost 500 schools in

Mid Glamorgan and each member of the partnership discusses teacher placements when they meet headteachers to discuss school/business links.

- Partnership members have many contacts in business. Once again while discussing school/business links they would ensure that the TPS is high on the agenda.

- The TPS is perceived by headteachers and business people as being part of a package of school/business activities. This gives it more relevance in the eyes of headteachers.

- Within Mid Glamorgan the partnership is seen as a quality organisation being supported by both the LEA and the business world. Being part of the partnership therefore gives the teacher placement organiser greater credibility.

- In Mid Glamorgan the teacher placement organiser is able to use the existing communication network to schools and business. This is efficient yet inexpensive. In addition publications produced by the partnership, such as its newspaper, include articles on teacher placements.

- The Partnership has strong links with other organisations and the teacher placement organiser is able to take advantage of this. Financial support has been secured from organisations which choose to be associated with programmes which feature teacher placements. Funds from the local Training and Enterprise Council, for example, have been made available to support schools participating in teacher placements.

As with other partnership programmes a small team has been assembled to oversee the Teacher Placement Service in Mid Glamorgan. This team consists of representatives of the Local Education Authority, Training and Enterprise Council and Partnership. The group meets each term to discuss strategy and targets. The members of this group are from senior management and therefore able to exert considerable influence within the Authority.

In conclusion the Teacher Placement Service is now an integral part of the Mid Glamorgan Education Business Partnership with the full weight of that organisation behind it. The role definition of the teacher placement organiser is not as clear as in most authorities but nevertheless an effective system of placing teachers to develop curriculum material or management expertise has been established.

The case study is typical of the TPS in action where priorities have been the developing of effective communication and the reinforcing of the concept of teams within teams.

The future of the Teacher Placement Service

The Teacher Placement Service continues to aim to provide placements in business for 10% of teachers per annum. The first two years of operation have been characterised by heavy marketing and promotion both locally and nationally in order to establish the concept with industry and education. The 20,000 placements achieved over this period have provided the basis of practice on which the service can now build, but it is important to move from externally driven activity to a school driven model. The priorities for the TPS are:

•   To integrate placements into the staff development plans of schools and the career profile of individual teachers. This must include the development of the ownership of the process at the school level, as a possible outcome of teacher appraisal. In so doing the quality of the service can be improved by ensuring that the objectives for individual placements are more closely related to the needs of the school and that there is support for implementing the outcomes of the experience.

•   For integration to be achieved it is important that the concept of teacher placement is introduced into the early years of teaching, as part both of the initial training and as induction into the local business community in the first teaching post. The induction of newly qualified teachers into the local education business community must be a priority for TPS with partnerships as these teachers will be potentially the most innovative, and the most important to influence at an early stage.

•   The most successful placement programmes to date have been developed from an identifiable need and developed into an accessible package which is clearly targeted with a prescribed framework e.g. *Women in Management, Transition from School to Work, Information Technology.* It is possible for such programmes to meet the objectives of organisations such as LEAs and TECs thus attracting additional funding.

•   There are specific difficulties affecting the primary sector such as the reduced ability to release teaching staff, the demands of National Curriculum implementation, a perceived lack of relevance and the priority given to the secondary sector by many companies. However, the quality of placement outcomes of primary teachers is of the highest standard, with evidence of significant curriculum programmes based on the placement experience. An increase in the number and proportion of primary placements will be a priority.

•   European placements as a means of strengthening European school/industry links, fostering cultural awareness, developing new curricular materials and enhancing language skills have been identified clearly through pilot programmes. The vision must be of a multi-lateral teacher placement programme between all community countries.

• The overwhelming priority has been given to teacher placements in industry whilst there have been excellent examples of reciprocal placement programmes placing business people into schools. The priority must be to increase the level of this activity.

The major challenge which has faced the Teacher Placement Service over the two years has been the issue of teacher release.

Despite market research[10] which indicates that over 81% of teachers are interested in the concept, it is the lack of an appropriate professional development model for teachers which provides the major limiting factor to future growth. The fact is that teacher release for professional development is cost intensive through supply cover and even with funds is very disruptive on the teaching process for young people. This problem goes beyond teacher placement activity, affects all forms of teacher professional development and inhibits the ability to maximise the potential that exists within the teaching profession.

Strategies to deal with this issue have been a major concern to local organisers. Funding for supply cover is available within the DES grants to LEAs for INSET, but in every case the demand for placements has outstripped the funds available, particularly given the competing demands that have existed within the LEAs' in-service programmes. However, as more funds have been devolved to schools, so the playing field has levelled out with headteachers making the decision on the basis of the potential return on the investment.

The fact that Teacher Placement Service has not had supply cover, although causing short term difficulties has improved the long term chances of success, as such additional external government funding would be temporary in nature. Instead it is because success has been dependent on the ability to win the argument on each individual placement with each headteacher that this investment, as part of the in-service programme, is worthwhile.

Conclusion

Teacher placement is a positive, worthwhile experience, personally and professionally, for education and business alike. The Teacher Placement Service both stimulates and is catalytic in the development of partnership activity. The TPS through its operation at the local level integrates initiatives such as Compact, SCIP, SATRO and other education business practitioners.

The weight of available evidence testifies to the direct and immediate worth of such individual experience for classroom and business alike by broadening the individual's outlook through:

- respect and recognition through increased knowledge of one another
- increased commitment to participation and continued involvement through increased communication
- change and adjustments to practice through problem solving and shared training
- exchange of resources
- personal understanding about the need for education business liaison
- refreshment and enhancement through the inspiration and motivation of community partners

This transformation of teachers' experiences is the key factor establishing the concept of partnership through direct experience. The Teacher Placement Service is partnership in action.

Appendix

Range of Support Materials produced:

- *UBI Guidelines for Teachers and Employers*
- *Teachers Into Business and Industry* — This Open University distance learning pack forms one module within the new Professional Development in Education Certificate for teachers undertaking accreditation.
- *Partnership in Learning: The Teacher Placement Service and the National Curriculum*, sponsored by Lloyds Bank, comprising guidelines which recognise the four key stages of the National Curriculum and address the core, foundation and cross-curricular themes.
- *The Primary Enterprise Pack* — This support pack has been developed especially for primary school teachers by the Polytechnic of North London.
- *Design Exchange* — The Teacher Placement Service, the Design Council and the Science and Technology Regional Organisation have collaborated to establish the Design Exchange.

● *Modern Languages Option In Industry Resources Pack* is available free to modern language teachers taking up a placement — a collaborative project between UBI, Barclays Bank, Department of Trade and Industry and Kent Education Authority.

● *Management Option* — The Teacher Placement Service has worked in partnership with Henley Distance Learning, Berkshire LEA, and Esso in producing a structured distance learning programme which includes the opportunity to examine management practice in business.

References

1 *Partnership: Working with Education*, DES, 1987.
2 DTI, Jan 1988, *White Paper*, Department for Enterprise.
3 UBI, Dec 1988, *Teacher Placement Programme 1988*.
4 CBI, *Introduction to Industry Scheme*, CBI Leaflet, 1983.
5 DES, Oct 1987, *Survey of school/industry links in Industry Year, 1986*.
6 CBI, Nov 1988, *Building a Stronger Partnership between Business and Secondary Education*. Report of the Confederation of British Industry Business Education, Task Force, London.
7 GEST Proposals, (Sept/Oct 90), Grants for Education Support and Training, DES.
8 Unpublished transcript, Duncan Graham, Chief Executive of National Curriculum Council, Jan 1990, Teacher Placement Service Conference, York.
9 King, B, Lea, C, Moroney, G, 1991, *The Partnership Handbook*, ED, p 92.
10 Andrew Irving Associates, May 1990, *DTI — Enterprise and Education Initiative — Teacher Trading Study*.

Section III

Chapter 9: A new role for partnerships

John Krachai

Partnerships between education and business are generally believed to be good, useful and worthwhile. The belief grows. It grows in particular communities and in the difficult-to-define territory of the national consciousness. Mutual benefits and shared learning are assumed to emanate from partnerships, predicated perhaps on the too simple notion that 'two plus two can make five'. Partnerships are about intentions but they derive their stature and attraction from what they achieve. The anticipation of new outcomes drives partnerships on. The desirability of close, productive, harmonious relationships between education and business is no longer questioned. The questions are about the scope and quality of partnership relationships. And of course it is through an examination of the quality and nature of relationships that the problematics arise.

Background: the growth of partnerships

The national movement for the establishment of Compacts demonstrates some of the problems. Young people are expected to engage in a 'contract' which, if fulfilled, entitles them to move more smoothly through a transition process between education and employment. Compacts are characterised by the establishment of targets for employers through job and training guarantees and for students (e.g. for attendance and punctuality though these are base targets and many targets are more sophisticated and driven by curriculum concerns). A sense of direction is clear — the outcomes are mutually agreed and explicit. However, it can be argued that the drive towards particular and explicit ends has actually limited what these partnerships could achieve. In the history of social improvement and development, compacts and other examples of 'limited' (e.g. 'feel good') partnership activities run the risk of being judged to be brief and enthusiastic failures.

There appears to be contradiction here; clearly partnerships, to be worth their invention and investment must have clear intended outcomes which are mutually understood. Even if the outcomes remain at the level of measurable behaviour the possibilities for partners to arrive at different interpretations of what has been 'agreed' are considerable. The scope for misunderstanding and the possibility of simply giving up the attempt increases hugely when the less tangible, less definable aims and outcomes of partnerships are considered. I believe there needs to be research into the development of hybrid organisations committed to education and training, yet distinct from the present notion of the school. Partnerships could be the host organisations for such research and development but this is likely to be regarded as too esoteric, too far from the pragmatic concerns of the immediate.

A national audit of the motivating forces behind partnership activities in the UK would indicate that they are presently embedded in economic philosophies and economic needs. These underpinnings of partnership activities in the UK at present are, I believe, dangerously narrow. They appear only to be concerned with the present and future quality of the labour market and the need to have a better and more highly trained workforce. The immediate economic imperatives have trapped the potential of partnerships which might otherwise attend to the more complex long-term issues and could therefore condition and shape our society in the future.

To summarise, many partnerships appear to have focused or been focused on the immediate and not necessarily the important. Frequently, the primary focus has been based on the supposed economic benefit of partnership rather than on educational — or learning — outcomes.

These opening remarks might be interpreted as a criticism of partnership activities. Not so. I hope they will allow access to hopes and expectations that partnerships can achieve profoundly important objectives which not only secure economic needs, but also transform how education is delivered, governed and perceived.

An analysis of the origins of partnerships, their supporters and sponsors, gives some important clues in the diagnosis of the development of partnerships to date. Partnerships in the UK are a contemporary feature; in their present incarnation they date from the mid 1980s and since then have grown remarkably into a national phenomenon. The majority of partnerships are based on a model imported from the USA and exemplified by the Boston Compact. Many partnerships have grown from this single root, nourished by central government and funded substantially, through a number of departments (particularly the Department of Trade and Industry and the Department of Employment; not, significantly, the Department of Education and Science). The Boston Compact was essentially about employability, (although there were some initial allusions to community regeneration); the two key funding UK government departments are obviously principally about the same thing.

There were, of course, antecedents to this recent surge of activity — notably, the Technical and Vocational Education Initiative (TVEI). That initiative articulated in very practical ways the need for the secondary school curriculum to become more relevant to the world of work. What distinguishes TVEI from current education business partnership activity is that, whilst it was conceptualised in the Department of Trade and Industry, it was nurtured largely within the educational community. Under TVEI, despite stimulating work experience programmes for students and industrial secondments for teachers, and a drawing together and integrating of previously disparate and competing activities (SCIP, Project Trident, SATROS), the real contacts between educators and the business community were essentially very limited. By contrast, recent partnerships have both parties equally active in pursuing their problematical objectives.

Prior to TVEI there was a remarkable absence of connectedness or dialogue between education and the business community. In the 1960s, for example, for a school or college to actively encourage teachers to discover more about business methods and practices was virtually unheard of. A clear characteristic of the English public education service has been its dislocation and separation from the business community. Indeed, many of the postures struck in the 19th century have been carried through to recent times; the belief, for example, that the educated do not enter business is still widespread, if not endemic in the national consciousness. Some sectors of industry, notably engineering, suffer from public attitudes which are still remarkably negative and ill-informed.

We have then, in the mid 1980s, a situation where two communities start to talk and meet with each other following a very long silence. Funds from government departments committed to trade and employment fuel their conversations. The ideas they discuss and promote centre on agreements between schools and businesses committed to achieving enhanced employability for students. The concepts and models are imported from the USA. The most widespread model in the UK is now being rejected in its country of origin. This rejection in the USA is coming partly as a result of the failure, as the business world sees it, of the education community to deliver increased, significant and measurable levels of attainment in the high school population. More importantly there is also now a distinct movement away from employability as the motive for partnership towards that of citizenship. This shift seems to have occurred as many in the business community observe what they interpret as the collapse of social order in American cities; a collapse, which carries with it the value systems underpinning the democratic state. In the USA in the 1990s there appears to be a wide recognition of the need to maintain the political system and these concerns are superceding previous motivations for partnerships.

What, then, should business and education be concerned with in their coming together in the UK in the 1990s? It is clear that one supplies labour and the other demands it, but do education and business have only this one thing in common? Current interpretations of partnership are surely running the risk of taking into account only the immediate when the advantage and purpose of partnerships is perhaps to do with something much more long term. It is with this potential of partnerships that the remainder of this chapter will be concerned.

As a starting point I want to examine some of the basic meeting points between the two communities — business and education — and some of their significant differences.

Education and business: meeting points

Perhaps the most obvious meeting point arises from some similarity in their organisation. Both operate within highly organised frameworks and infrastructures. Until quite recently the 'Head Office' of the education service was the local education department with schools and colleges as the 'production sites'.

Both also depend on their human capital. For business the notion that employees are the most valuable 'capital item' is relatively recent, though it is now widely accepted. Within education there has been the long standing view that the individual teacher is the key resource to developing and delivering a high quality service.

Nationally, what both education and business produce is valued and thought to be of vital importance. An indication of this importance can be seen in the inclusion of economic awareness and industrial understanding as a cross curricular theme in the National Curriculum. The proposal is intended to allow students access to understanding business more fully through core and foundation subjects. Increasingly, then, there is a recognition that the products of education and business are the twin pillars on which a contemporary market led economy will stand.

If certain organisational features, their dependence on the human resource and their national recognition are all points in common, differences between them may be more marked, more extensive and more culturally deep rooted.

Business and education: divergence

The purpose — what education and business variously set out to do — is perhaps the most useful point at which to start. Whilst there are a number of interpretations, the basic purpose of business in our society is to generate profits and create wealth. Emanating from this comes a range of other imperatives concerned with social and employment conditions but, without a positive balance sheet, the business community can achieve nothing. The purpose of education, expressed through a single description, is even more problematic. Perhaps it is not possible to reduce it to a single definition, but for the purpose of this passage I will concentrate on the individual learner. In these terms, the purpose of education is to enable the individual to lead a fulfilling and productive life. But in reality the particular focus of education is neither clear nor controllable; rather there is a complex of objectives determined as best by a galaxy of interested parties — there is no real consensus.

The criteria for evaluation of 'success' in the two domains are also very different. Business parameters are set by the market; the focus is the customer or client and their demands. In education there is a diffused sense of the customers. Who are they? Parents, students or the community? The growth of business is subject to market forces: these determine growth or contraction, success or failure. In education, the sense of direction, and the evaluation of its various purposes, is subject to national and local policies with political imperatives providing the stimulus for change. The business community recognises that those enterprises deemed to be successful are those which are responsive to market changes. For education, on the other hand, there is a greater degree of constancy in what it aims to do — a constancy, underpinned by philosophies and political ideals of long-standing. Successful business has an inbuilt ability to change rapidly, whether it be in terms of identifying new markets and expectations or diversifying from customer bases. Education, on the other hand, is slow to change, discernible change being measurable in years, or even decades. If they are unsuccessful, businesses close, they simply no longer exist. If education is unsuccessful who, in any short term sense, knows that that is the case? Only in the most extreme cases does any sense of closure pertain. Performance is relatively easy to measure and understand in the business community. Performance in education is complex, controversial and should properly be set in the context of long time scales.

Important organisational features extend the catalogue of difference between business and education. Business has a varied set of formats, from public to private ownership, from board-dominated to the locally-owned small operation. Education, on the other hand, is a public service without a keen sense of direct ownership and is managed by an agglomeration of national and local groups. At least this was so until very recently, though the effects of the 1988 Education Reform Act (ERA) may have begun to change things.

Differences are very stark as well as in relation to accountability. Business operates on clear lines of accountability — the public company through its board to the shareholders, the small business to the directors or the individual owner. In education the chains of accountability are long, complex and at times tangled with national and local political groups, senior management teams, governing bodies and education officials all of whom have some responsibility in the accountability process.

Finally, examination of the power bases for education and for business signals further crucial difference. Power in business is derived from confidence, a confidence drawn from the balance sheet, by the generation of wealth. The powerful company is a rich company and the powerful business person is successful in that particular context. Power through wealth and confidence leads into the upper echelons of companies and into networks and lobby groups which have an ability to extend influence into other domains in our society through elite networks. This power, and its influence, is discernible and easily located in terms of its roots and usage. By contrast, education as a system derives its power from a legal, rational understanding that it constitutes an essential social service. From this understanding springs a whole edifice, a complex hierarchy dominated by political processes, the power of national and local government, the powers of the governing body, the powers of the senior management team of the school or college. One invests the other. Power trickles down the edifice with the effect that those who actually deliver the service, teachers and lecturers, are the least powerful in terms of determining what the service is about, how it performs, how it should develop.

If, then, business and education are so very different — what chance is there of realisation in practice of the theoretical potential of partnerships? These fundamental dissimilarities will surely militate against the two communities coming together. Perhaps what they are doing at present is coming together on issues that are essentially unproblematic and secure whilst leaving the deep differences untouched. In other words they are continuing to operate in their separate ways, largely untouched one by the other.

Realising the potential: what education might learn from business

This essential separation means that the full potential will not be realised. I believe that essential dimensions and indeed products are possible through a conflation of business and education, producing new paradigms for the creation of new forms of understanding, new structures, new entities and new ideas. New, for what purpose? Education is currently undervalued, under-achieving and under-resourced in the UK and requires a fundamental and radical transformation. It may be that, over time, education can take a long term view of itself through the medium of the successful business. For it is within successful business practice that the ability to think and plan long-term is found.

I want now to look more closely at how business operates and see if in that operation there are any lessons, ideas or strategies that might be the beginnings of the new direction for education. Specifically, by considering the themes of adaptability, accountability and technological coherence I believe we have principles and processes by which business might prompt the education service to question and change its own practices.

Adaptability and accountability

Successful businesses are highly adaptable — they demonstrate an ability to change rapidly in response to market demands, client needs and public perceptions. Clearly all organisations, if they are to be successful need to adapt to changed circumstances. What distinguishes business in terms of adaptability is the consequences if adaptation, and in some cases rapid adaptation, does not occur — signal failure. This ability to move quickly, whilst retaining an integrity in terms of structure and direction, may be a clue for the future. A further clue may lie in the interpretation of accountability in the business world. Here accountability is clearly defined, the routes and paths through which it flows are easily discerned, often articulated and condition the nature, state and integrity of the whole enterprise.

Adaptability in business may require organisational or structural change on a grand scale — the skills and procedures to achieve such change are learnt, not automatically available. An emerging contemporary example of radical change is in the business which to date has been concerned with the defence industries. With the changes in the political environment and the climate globally and continentally, some companies which have grown and built their considerable business on the production of arms now find themselves in a changed situation; many have moved very rapidly to the formulation of new products and services quite distinct from their original product base. Other examples involve key business sectors responding to national and international competition by devising radically new management structures. 'Flat topping' has become an evident feature of business change — it describes organisational structures where hierarchies have been reduced and the number of levels between the managing director and the shop floor have become fewer. The intention is to facilitate better communication and a greater sense of ownership and sharing. Many of these management structures and processes have long histories — quality circles and Japanese corporate practice are two trends which influence current thinking in business management aspirations, expectations and structures. To occasion change, then, requires a willingness to respond to changed perceptions, and changed circumstances. It requires a 'learning culture', an expectation and anticipation that the business world does not stand still, because it cannot.

Anticipation is an essential ingredient in good business practice; it is one of the mainsprings that drives a successful business on. The trend in a number of large corporate structures to remove layers of management to allow better communication and a clearer view of what is actually going on at the productive base is recognition that clear, unambiguous communication is a further mainspring in developing an organisation. Communication is the fuel which drives accountability. Messages are clearer, misunderstandings are fewer when communication systems have a minimum of 'filters'. By contrast, complex systems, with many filters offer the probability of obfuscation and abuse.

I should make it clear that I am drawing on notions of an *idealised* business environment when I refer to unambiguous communication being the motive power which occasions accountability Many businesses in the UK within the multi national conglomerates — business entities with huge work-forces and sophisticated products and services — have clear pathways through which people understand their responsiblities and the parameters for discharging that responsibility. In education, by contrast, even in the post ERA environment the classroom teacher, directly accountable for the progress or otherwise of student learning, has a bewildering multi-layered system of accountability to wade through. This encompasses government imperatives as well as the management systems of the LEA and the school — it ensures that any clear sense of accountability, on the part of those at the 'production base' is improbable.

Accountability operates in the same domain as trust. Responsibility for those who deliver the education service requires people to feel and to know that they have a professional responsibility and can be trusted to discharge that. Partnerships might prompt the education service to take a closer look at those businesses which have reformed their communication strategies and their managerial structures to allow more direct links with the client. With the reforms underway in terms of local financial management such connections might be made more easily.

Adaptability and accountability, then, are two key features that the best of the business community knows and understands.

Technological coherence

A third key feature is technology. It is obvious that business activity would falter and collapse without the use and constant development of information/data-based technologies. Not only does business continue to demand exploration in technological development, it completes the cycle by voraciously consuming its applications. Technology, as many successful businesses show, become the means and the ends. This continuing cycle, or perhaps more appropriately spiral, is clearly visible in those industries which centre on electronics and are in the business of producing robots and artificial intelligences which go with them. It is in these environments that there is evidence of real ability to anticipate the future and plan responses in a systematic way.

Education as a complex process could do well to recognise and learn from the business community in this whole massively expanding area. In the UK the use of technology has been *ad hoc*, weak and generally insufficient. Students in schools are too often exposed to 19th century technology (paper-bound administration systems, blackboards and chalk) yet in their homes many have learnt to become competent in the technologies of the 20th century. It appears, at times that there is an unbridgeable gap between what contemporary business uses and what the school does. There must come a point when educators and business leaders share and learn about the transferability of technology from one domain to another.

An enhanced role for partnerships

I want to argue that partnerships should actively begin to research into the best of business practice, understand what it is about and create structured opportunities for education to learn, transfer and absorb. This naturally raises a number of crucial questions: what is the best, how is it discerned? Is it possibly transferable to education and, given that teachers, lecturers and senior management teams are slow to change, can rapid change, in any event, ever be characteristic of a social service?

I would suggest that the best business venture is one that values the individual explicitly, that attends to individuals outside their immediate task and determined function. The best also requires clear communication systems which allow the individual to share some of the power and take part in decision making. Lastly, the best refers to business which values ideas and creativity, which stimulates and encourages individual development, particularly in terms of recognising that the individual does not represent one set of potentials but many. Individuals frequently work in a number of different company environments and experience a steady stream of training and personal development.

The best businesses are characteristically adaptable to changing circumstance, a state which depends on individuals being encouraged and stimulated into being learners with the confidence to adapt positively. Norm referenced measures of learning, always a dominant, presently an overbearing, influence on the education scene, do little to encourage this approach to human development in both student and teacher populations.

Much of the potential for transferability of good practice could come through a series of innovations which partnership might originate, provided it is prepared to transcend traditional structures. The first innovation would come in the form of more direct access to development budgets, allowing re-prioritisation towards a greater teacher immersion into some of the business practices outlined above.

Clearly, with the arrival of local financial management, this directness of budgetary control and prioritisation can occur, provided there is enough money in the system. The second innovation can come, in this post ERA environment, by a steady reformulation of management systems and structures within schools and colleges — a version of flat topping, of stripping out the layers of management and the filters through which messages can be confused and made more complex. This whole approach would not necessarily require an immersion into the business environment but could draw on partnerships as a clearing house for the illumination and dissemination of the best practice around. Much is now available to the individual school or college, in terms of adapting management structures, since the control of the LEA is reduced and responsibility for innovation and change lies with the institutions. However, resources are required for these opportunities for education to learn and adapt business approaches.

Given the growing acceptance of the view that education represents the basic condition for future economic success, partnerships are surely well placed within their localities to begin the task of building the structures and confidence necessary to establish education investment banks or funds where there is a professional approach given to venture capital for educational development. This would be managed by those with an understanding that research and development are investments which produce a return, not merely a cost. This return should be expressed through performance of the individual learning site, the criterion for what is successful being a comprehensive record of achievement and experience, not a battery of inert test scores.

I have mentioned in passing the potential advantages for schools and colleges with the arrival of the Education Reform

Act (1988). Perhaps present arrangements make accountability more complex and confused than in the recent past but, through partnerships in communities, and a growing sense and confidence that schools and colleges are capable of managing their own affairs, it is entirely possible that the problems of accountability can be resolved.

Here partnerships would not act as a proxy or alternative to the local education authority but rather as facilitators, allowing schools and colleges to learn more about accountability, how it is portrayed and realised.

The education community urgently needs a new framework for local strategic planning and accountability. Opted-out schools, operating in atomised isolation, in competition with each other and with the rump of the LEA system are unlikely to be capable of collective action in support of whole community needs. A local system approach to the provision of schooling will continue to be important, especially in urban areas. Community provision demands community accountability, disappearing fast in practice with the demise of the LEA. What is needed is a structure which encourages accountability and quality assurance in the service of local need.

One of the problems of LEA control has been that local government is a highly politicised domain. Parties compete for local power and with national government. Adversarial activity is what calls local government into being. The combative ethic of politics is inappropriately placed at the centre of the governance of education, which desperately needs to be guided by the values of partnership.

There is a crucial role for partnerships in taking on responsibility for the local co-ordination of education. The TECs come nearest to this aspiration in their potential for fostering a partnership ehtic within a framework of accountability and sound systems management. It may be necessary to extend representation more equitably beyond the domination of business interests so that more insights into community need might find expression. At the very least TECs have a vital role in researching and developing an operating model for the creation of local education strategies which could bring some strategic order to an otherwise rapidly fragmenting school system.

These claims place partnerships in a new and crucial role. Educational establishments, through partnerships need to research into supportive evaluative procedures, to simplify lines of accountability and to attend to issues of quality in education. Secondly it is essential that learning establishments begin to understand how organisational adaptability occurs. Thirdly a real and sustainable push is necessary on the use of technology, not just in the administration of education but in its use to augment the role of the teacher. This amounts to a technology which liberates not only the teacher but the learner and allows both to make more intelligent connections between the worlds of school and the wider community. The role of the teacher could be expanded to encompass the role of researcher. This refocusing could come about by individual students following particular pathways determined by them in negotiation, not only with teachers, but also with mentors in the business and wider communities. This implies a decline in the role of the school as the sole agent of the delivery of education, and the emergence of new organisational entities nourished by partnerships. It is in this future that perhaps partnerships can be seen for what they are, a new kind of relationship in which power is shared rather than used to fight others. Partnerships are a radical intervention in a world stuck with its past, confounded by its present and fearful of its future.

Chapter 10: Assertion of the North — partnership for regional development

Michael Harrison

St William's Foundation and the North of England

The thesis of this chapter is that the North of England is in urgent need of modern development. St William's Foundation (the northern cousin of St George's House, Windsor Castle, and like it an independent, voluntary institution) was established recently with the major remit of addressing just this issue. The Foundation's new strategy starts with a broad review of the Northern environment[1], in the context of a UK with many strengths but also considerable weaknesses.

Absolutes aside, it is clear that relative to other advanced industrial countries Britain's economy has grown for too long less sturdily. Overall levels of education and of skills are lower, our institutions are coping only fitfully with modern conditions and there is an unsafely low level of investment.

If these broad observations of Britain are true, then the North of England has similar deficiencies, with added handicaps. St William's Foundation sees the need for a programme of action which will explore new paths, side step old obstacles, find lateral avenues to solution of apparently intractable problems. It seeks above all to help into being a multi-level network of partnerships. A continuously low level of investment for many years has stunted the possibility of the 'First Industrial Revolution' turning into a 'Second'. Rail and road links are inadequate, especially the connections across the Pennines with the single exception of the M62 (the national assumption in 1991 being that the Roman system radiating from London is still good enough). Northern society is dominated by such physical facts — also by two centuries of poor health, low expectation, isolation and undervaluation. The depth and complexity of problems to be overcome begin to be apparent. Furthermore, while in former times the responsible authorities strove their hardest to mitigate poverty, of circumstance and opportunity, by driving hard for high levels of education provision, low expectation still depressed educational achievement, and work-related training in industry continued to be low-grade — where employers allowed it to happen at all. And so a malign circle developed — unlike the ascending spiral occurring in more southerly parts. The economic and social system was locked.

Failure of institutions

Attitudes of successive governments so far have only solidified the lock. The institutions of economic, social and community development invented in the nineteenth century have kept pace with neither need nor aspiraion. The environment of our society, relative to others of its kind, looks threadbare. The public infrastructure founded years ago when we felt rich patently does not deliver a quality of service we think we deserve — just at the time we realise we are not as rich as we thought. A serious decline of leadership in local affairs compounds the difficulty. Ideology pulling hither and thither — sometimes resulting in apparent loss of direction — has not helped.

Government in early 1991 proposed reform of local government, but it was not clear then how far a strident need to deal with local government financing dominated the intent. The North of England could be forgiven scepticism. With more resources needed to remedy long neglect, let alone raise quality of environment to modern standards, and with government bearing down on public expenditure, it is the North of England with its inherited urban-industrial burdens that suffers the most. When restrictions curtail northern education programmes (as recently) on which so much hope for the future must depend, then the North seems clear victim to central government's lowering of its economic and social prospects. Balanced against the North's previous sacrifices in the cause of the common wealth, this is treatment scarcely to be borne.

Failure of centralism

Thrown by the conundrum of local government finance, government finds no easy solutions to the underlying issues of central-local relationships — those questions of the economic and political 'assignments' that a satisfactory condition of democracy requires. The massive effort of the 1970s Royal Commission is to be followed by yet another enquiry. True, the scenery has changed. For instance, government may have gained some pilot experience in attracting private money and management into certain areas like urban redevelopment and water resources. In larger economic terms, however, some previous attempts at intervention in the regions have been misguided, even patronising, assuming the North best supported by being kept in its place and in the (terminal) condition it should expect. The result — heavy industry and low value added production kept going long past its time, ineffectually, by subsidy.

The North might well observe too that it would rather be free of national economic policies that have only succeeded, over so many post-war years and through several alternating governments, in bringing the country to a level of GNP per head visibly falling behind all our respectable rivals — and some newcomers till recently beneath notice.

Failure of vision

In short, the centralism of the day seems a prop without much worth. Depriving localities of many of their powers and discretions, encouraging through 'nannying' from the centre a dependency culture in the provinces, the national government — locked in its own record of multi-sided failure — simply maintains a self-justifying authority.

Yet this authority sees no alternative to itself. The provincial landscape of factions and fractions — localities squalling in impotence, absurdly competing for crumbs of resources, with no incentive to collaborate — is of course its own creation. It then complicates matters further by promoting voluntarism in a market that can only imperfectly express itself.

'Anti–statist' ideas of consumerism and individual citizen responsibility may be respectable enough, but government seems to have not much further to say — beyond a vaguely humanitarian appeal to the 'social market': it develops as yet publicly no vision of coherent aims, no serious analysis of pressing social and economic issues, their territories and their boundaries, no perception of the system flexibility that could satisfy both ideology and the real national need for effective progress.

No wonder that the North of England feels itself still left in the dark.

A platform of advantage

Does it seem impossible to escape from the dauntingly sticky web of difficulty outlined above? The national centre, exhausting its ingenuity and conventional values, has little new to offer. But the North of England, midway between the nation state and its local fractions, may be seen as a unit seriously equipped for self-sufficiency. This essay is not going to speculate on notions of devolved regional government — a subject for another day. The three-region Northern Province however is in the bigger league of population — large enough, as already mentioned, to stand international comparison. In size and character it matches regions on the Continent qualifying for European Community special regional status, which smaller areas scarcely do. Of course there are differences among the three northern regions — and not inconsiderable distances, from Doncaster to the Border and from North to Irish Seas. Yet there is here in the English highland zone an ancient Brigantian unity, later distinguished by the northern capital of the Roman Empire at York, concreted by the establishement of the boundary of Mercia-Northumbria and the specifically Norse occupation. While East-West links across the Pennines are not good enough for the modern world, there are still the time-honoured facilitating gaps of Tyne and Aire, now complemented by the M62.

A northern sense of identity concentrated by the frustration of spirit that knows it could manage better what its southern overseers only botch is pressure enough for a new drive for progress.

Prospects for growth

Growth would not start from scratch, without a legacy. Precedents have been set by the Trans-Pennine Movement (with an all-party MPs' group in support), by the powerful counter-action in the North East when Scottish devolution was in the air; the developmental spirit of the regional economic planning councils abolished by government in 1979 is abroad again, though unconnected, in all three regions. The North has a positive disproportion of higher education institutions, and so the intellectual power of centres of research. Its natural environment, its four national parks, its recreational facilities are supremely attractive — just the sort of advantage exploited in America some years ago in the model high-tech regeneration of Georgia and the Carolinas.

The talents and adaptability, the grit, the robustness of its people are legendary. They are a work force crying out for engagement and reward, a force moreover that from its roots understands the value of technical skills, and of education allied to technology. If westerly trade has declined, prospects to the east are bright. The East Coast ports from the Humber to the Tyne are now an obvious gateway to fast-growing trade with the rest of the European Community, and to potential growth areas in recently liberated Eastern Europe. Traffic congestion in the South East encourages new links across the North Sea. Leeds is emerging as the second most important financial centre in England. The scene is set.

Partnership

An initiative

The libretto now needs writing, not in terms of expectation of aid from elsewhere — little will come — but expressing the room for the innate, self-help strengths of local people and communities. St William's Foundation here offers itself as latter-day *deus ex machina*. Independence allows it to try new parts that others may not be able to play. Its quest is for an active invention of a whole pattern of 'effective partnerships', to help Northerners and northern agencies of all kinds to work together in a co-operative of enlightened self-interest.

Panorama and hypothesis

The Foundation's broad survey, relating world-wide events to the condition and future of the North of England, attempts to show how the Northern home of the Industrial Revolution, which changed the course of civilisation, can earn a reflex benefit from the outside world: to suggest how it should see its continuing importance and the integrity of its peculiar contribution to that world, the value of its own inalienable strengths and their potential.

This broad panorama brings with it a number of effects. First, it deliberately sets out to extend the North's horizons and raise its sights, believing thus that is internal vision will expand.

However, the opening attempt at such a panorama, even if well observed, can only be provisional. But it should be lively enough to engage the interest and the future assistance of better analysts.

Its very provisionality though is to be stressed. A snapshot panorama will constantly, sometimes strikingly, be overtaken by unforeseen events.It is a graphic hypothesis, expecting to be tested by succeeding stages of effort.

Lastly, it make the base for construction of a large scenario — a first short at identifying, with least danger of short sight (though perhaps roughly drawn in the first stages), the major issues to be treated as priorities for action. Definition of priorities empowers the next stage — an action plan. This can be expected to attack priorities first at the most expeditious points, where ground is favourable and forces ready. Most importantly, the first (and indeed later) sallies are always related to the framework erected by survey, scenario and plan.

A whole North partnership?

If a national style of thinking and intention openly presented, with results of action always revealed, became a large scale, habitually public act, it alone would be a considerable achievement. Issues vital to the well-being and future of individuals and communities broadcast on a new level of information and sophistication would mark a big step forward for thoughtful democracy. To have involved the whole North of England in a continuing search for knowledge, with hypothesis and verification conducted in the best Popperian manner, would be a signal development in community maturity.

So St William's invites itself for adoption as the first party to a partnership in a universal sense. The invitation makes no declaration of superior knowledge, it demands no acceptance of a higher authority. Its aim is, through the getting together of the highest quality of thinking and perception, to become an unstoppably persuasive force to others in alliance. The complementary side of this partnership of thinking is composed of all those willing to join in the intellectual effort with the energy that it calls for. From that moment of acceptance a partnership in principle is in business.

The nature of partnership

'Partnership' is a powerful concept. It carries a multitude of meanings and possibilities. It embodies the collaborative, team approach. From all concerned parties it invites commitment, which eliminates negativism. Commitment leads on to a feeling of responsible ownership, and then pride. Involvement in partnership optimises human ability and resource, neglects nothing that could add value, produces a synergy of intellect and vigour. It can help to identify problems with clarity, and find specific remedies to meet them. In local situations it leads to mutual respect between generations and among different sectors and levels of society. It can not only focus a desire for action, but is also satisfyingly accurate in its local 'fine-tuning'. Partnership avoids the dysfunction of other forms of human organisation — the contingent frictions, hostilities and invented obstacles. It is a means to achievement.

All partnership are voluntary. They can be close or loose, highly defined or only vaguely so, even to the point of being implicit. In all cases the partnership contract carries mutual recognition of value and interest. Partnership may turn out to have a relatively long life but are not formed on that expectation. With time and experience their character will evolve. There would indeed be danger in an assumption of permanence. Permanence implies rules and rigidities; structures so tight must risk becoming mechanistic. Partnership bureaucratised carries with it the seeds of its own corruption.

But, to borrow ideas from Professor Charles Handy[2], partnership should still strive for its own immortality. It will achieve this not through seeing itself as a piece of concrete, proprietary estate, as an end in itself; rather it is a moving organisation for progress, existing for its future not its present, and achieving its future, and so fulfilling its *raison d'etre*, in aspiration for, and achievement of, improvement. Its own agreement to exist as a partnership is its investment in its own future effectiveness. Its parties are bonded to each other for this purpose, choosing as they will how to express the contract.

Its life is bound up with the achievement of tasks or programmes, and is realised through them. These are strictly temporary events, working as self-evaluating systems. Their success, and if appropriate their renewal in the form of tasks and programmes informed by feedback from their predecessors, is what justifies the partnership and validates its integrity.

Their ephemeral character is the essence of the 'un-permanence' of the partnership that bore them. The temporariness of the task is, by definition, contained in its nature; the temporariness of the partnership is derived from the task which binds it. And the partnership's life is a short as a task completed or as long as a connected, improving spiral of programme sustains it through renewal.

Contributors

If a scenario for action is to be socially and politically acceptable in an area it has to be linked into people's beliefs about their present positions and purposes. In its future strategy St William's has to liaise with many existing institutions and agencies, at higher or lower levels. Each of them will have its own integrity, its own remit and its belief in its own purpose. Many, like local authorities, will have a constitutional status.

But in addition the strategy demands initiation of many local groups. In soliciting response to analysis and subsequent proposals produced out of higher level partnerships, it would be asking for local ideas to be contributed to the whole. Local groups, joined in a network, together and with St William's and its agents, should be not only validators of priorities; they should also become centres of influence and information in local communities, in a stronger position than ever before to influence institutional government. So, the result should move in the direction of an open information society and away from the oligarchic tendencies to be seen in much political party management of local discussion.

Partnership and networks

Establishment of partnership relationships will occur at three main levels:

- for intelligence purposes, with agencies willing to ally their resources for analysis and research to the common framework. Their findings would go to reinforce or modify it. Higher education institutions and their research institutes are clear candidates for partnership (and initial links are already being made). Others will be in centres of regional development, local authorities and commerce. Their value will lie in their willingness to share intelligence in the common Northern interest.
- secondly, among regional development associations, local authorities, urban development corporations and the like. Voluntary and professionally based organisations too will have valuable contributions to make (organisations like the Society of Education Officers and the regional organisations of the Engineering Council come to mind). These exist already, though few of them inter-regionally.
- at a third level of support, the local groups already mentioned, generally interested in local development and

connecting to the special interests of e.g., LEAs, TECs, Chambers of Commerce.

It would be part of the Foundation's role in partnership at all levels to encourage development of networks where they do not already exist, and to reinforce them where they do — for greater consolidated strength and continuous intercommunication. Throughout, there would be constant iteration of information. Partnerships would be fed with, and themselves would feed, to and fro, data, experience and insights into and out of a web of reliable intelligence.

Tasks and programmes

Progressive emergence of partnership forces, combined with provisional intentions and priorities, will clear the ground for tasks and levels of partnership at which they could be set to be identified. Tasks, leading into programmes, will be arranged against the reference of the framework, varying infinitely in depth or extent, contributing no only to localised progress but also as part of the whole Northern interest.

Tasks or programmes need to be treated as 'temporary systems' — that is, operations with defined objectives, internal plans for action, linked to scales of time and resource, with built-in mechanisms for monitoring progress and evaluating results — a cardinal principle at every level. It is to be accepted that tasks and programmes will have the character of 'experimental action', and some of the experiment will fail, or end up with results different from those expected.

The 'systematic approach' needs to be complemented by a methodical collection and storage of information, which beyond its operational value can be developed and presented, without loss of standard, to appeal to the media. The Foundation initiative needs the continuous interest of the press in all its guises, to bring it regularly to public attention, to raise awareness, the level of sophistication of concern, cross-fertilising enthusiasms. In its way, the relationship between the initiative and the press is another form of partnership — and it should be managed in that light.

A new form of management

Such a structure of partnership and network bespeaks delicate handling. It cannot be in any sense hierarchical. The term 'management' may have too many inherited connotations, perhaps of arrogation of command, of assumption of superiority. One party to partnership cannot be 'owned' and so driven by another; each has equal status, in the nature of the reciprocal contract. Management of a kind there must be however, for maintenance of direction and purpose of the whole provincial operation. St William's has presented itself as a prime mover and so it falls to St William's to work out how to express itself as a managing agent. It will be cultivating new ground; the scale and complexity envisaged is daunting. The Foundation must aim to build up and then maintain energy and momentum by exploiting the moral authority of its position as insistent 'animateur'.

Priority themes

Watershed: a view from the ridge

The guiding line of St William's initial panorama is that the beginning of the decade of the 1990s marks off a new era. The convergence of geopolitical events, of the consequences of the technology that has been fermenting in the post-war years, of new ideologies, of government processes are of a scale and significance unprecedented for half a century. They demand radical reassessments from agencies like the Foundation with strategic aspiration.

Review throws up three vast sectoral changes. One is political and economic; it is represented by the discrediting of Communism, the dubious future of the Russian Empire, the end of the dangerous age of the polarised superpowers: with, in parallel, failing American confidence in its economy and culture faced by the rising economic power of the Pacific Basin. The second is the potential of the European Community as a unified trading and political bloc, with the accelerating prospect, stimulated by the collapse of the Iron Curtain, of a 'greater Europe'. The third is a less tangible but no less striking phenomenon, the general feeling for freedom that has come over us all, an understanding heightened by the recent escape of millions of people by 1990 from the miseries of authoritarian rule and command economies. But it is also part of that long revolt in more liberal climes against the dominance of the 'providing state', along with the rise of the individual citizen consumer — Galbraith's 'politics of comfort'. These great events, the *zeitgeist* mood they engender, large in themselves as stages in history, carry with them an enormous potential for change in our daily lives. If past experience is any guide, the present engines of administration and leadership will only sluggishly meet the pressure of the occasion. Britain's systems are good at coping with specific emergencies — not so good at dealing with long developing crisis, but no less explosive for its slow fuse.

So if things are to be done quickly, an approach able to look without let or hindrance at problems, even the most deep-seated, is needed: to define them in the clearest terms: to suggest alternative ways to solutions: finally, to seek resources for those solutions. Such a search will involve itself of course with received institutions; certainly it will go beyond them. The resources needed will not come easily, but tasks defined in partnership can be expected to unlock new stores, not neccessarily the most conventional, of energy and material.

Priorities

What are the urgencies? They all derive from those larger issues already mentioned. The economy is the prime subject — followed by a parcel of supporting elements — strongly connected to the issues of technology and education. These three themes named are vital in any real future for the North. Marking up the priorities is the first step to consideration of the means to attack them.

1. The economy

It comes as the central priority because without a successful economy nothing else prospers. The whole country has a huge negative balance of visible trade, its manufacturing (and exporting) industry weakened and its range dangerously uncomprehensive, too much characterised by low added value. But the North's recent comb-out of traditional industries leaves it with an imbalanced legacy and serious economic handicap. On top of that, its infrastructure is inadequate, its management weak, its human resources underexploited, its R & D potential neglected.

2. Central-local affairs

After much experiment we still have no satisfactory resolution of our local government problem. The international trend is towards an ever greater degree of devolution; here the tendency has been to centralise, and the issues of autonomy, which most locals want, are confused with the mechanics of finance. Intertwined are questions of national standards (as in aspects of education, policing, environmental control) and the mode of delivery in which standards are set. Different scales of provision (transport for locality or large city, community schools or further education) may be better for different systems. A variety of flexible solutions may apply in different places. Is the uniformity we have come to expect necessary? Today's citizens deserve the chance to speak radically on how they want to be governed locally today.

One large illustration — when the health of the North's economy needs new pace in education and training, to be hobbled by forms and structure dictated by the centre is unjustifiable. National criteria can stimulate; national control will deaden.

3. Infrastructure

Northern distances, as always, ask for particular care about transport and communications. This means a network of modern highways, high-speed trains, airports and air routes, superior facilities for passenger and freight handling — and telecommunications that support the management of trade. The focus of the country's trade, already with the European Community, will shift again with new freedom in Eastern Europe. The Northern opportunity for all kinds of commerce across the North Sea intensifies. It needs support from agents of investment, further exploitation of its special off-shore position as a base for international funds. Its workforce needs rapid improvement to suit, its management levels and vision upgrading. Its centres of analysis and research need positively gearing to the task, entailing the high quality staff, institutions and supporting education structure neccessary for such facilities to thrive in situ.

4. Renewal

The North has had more than its fair share of the squalor of industrial inheritance. Built, physical environment have an inevitable cycle of decay — equally inescapable for non-physical institutions. Without renewal, decay becomes irredeemable. Decayed environments invite bulldozers and wholesale demolition — antithesis of the process of replacement over generations that gives so many townscapes in Britain their appeal. Decay lowers morale in communities, even to rock-bottom, equating with levels of grinding poverty — inescapable, and classic breeding ground for so much anti-social behaviour including crime.

Structures of management and finance devised to maintain environments and institutions may not be the same as are needed to oversee renewal. Different attitudes are required, capable of rising above and not being muddled by the pressing detail of daily affairs, bringing broad experience and greater discrimination to bear on planning and development issues.

5. Enterprise

The 'enterprise culture' has taken hold. It accords with today's ideology of individualism. It succeds the corporatism of the 1970s and 1980s, it coincides with the growth of the idea of small profit centres. It has parallels in the 'education for capability' movement, and in the general modern response in education to the call for self-sufficient individuals, suitably equipped as adults to be project managers, team workers, problem solvers. It is the necessary foundation for growth of small businesses. But it needs complementary mechanisms for counselling, transmission of experience, management expertise, financial support, upskilling programmes. At the earliest stage it should be made to come alive for young people and teachers in the processes of education.

6. Technology

Modern technology is a prime determinant of economic growth. The international experience is obvious. The North, if it does not accelerate up-market into high-tech areas of design and production, will become lost and stagnant. These new areas have to be identified and realised. Northern distance — given development of communications — need be no object, as witness the Forth-Clyde Valley resurrection. High-tech advance however is not feasible without a highly qualified manpower stock. Engineering innovation, creative design, technology transfer, technician support — all these in turn depend upon an education and training effort recognising economic urgency.

7. Education and training

The subject is now, properly, top of politicians' agenda. Populist pressure demands higher standards in the basics. These are indeed vital, but overconcern about them obscures wider issues. High national standards overall entail three more very large developments.

First comes extension of educational ideas and curriculum countering low aspirations and expectations present in too many Britons, bred in them by a century and more of patronising neglect. Secondly, we desperately need a comprehensive structure of opportunity and provision for the 16–19 age groups. Curing the deficiency in this area, thirdly, is the necessary base for a much larger proportion of our age groups than at present (about 15%) to go on to advanced education — in both academic and especially applied studies. In addition, wider and more varied forms of higher education opportunity must be devised to enable the expansion needed.

Our competitors — who use their better provision of education to beat us at the economic game — show us how a slender force of educated human resources, our current situation, is no basis for technical expertise in volume, for high intellect in commerce, for leadership quality in management, or for any other human component of economic success.

Questions of training are connected. Training structures in an industrial setting where targets and aspirations are underpitched have thin prospects. In a low-tech environment, under a depreciated view of industrial performance, where management vision is poor, product-related training does not appear urgent. A situation like this continues only at the peril of all of us, and a heavy responsibility rests on the new TECs to set it right.

Into action

These priority themes are notable for their deep-textured interconnection. There is scarely an element of any that is not linked to another. It demonstrates the imperative that solid forward progress will depend on action taken across the broad front of endeavour. There will be many elements to action, but the whole should be systematic.

Interconnection of elements determine that action can only run effectively in a matrix. One category of activity cross-references with others, reinforcing the original St William's strategic framework idea. Military operation — not the battle but the campaign — offers analogy. In it reconnaissance leads on to strategy and related tactics; there is management of logistics and intelligence, of time as well as of forces; planning is constantly updated by observation and reporting; field actions have their own integrity, but are kept in tune with the master plan.

Partnership for survival

Partnership in operation can release physical and financial resources that otherwise would remain obscured. Every morsel of support to be found needs to be brought into play. Originating with employment and education issues, now the partnership concept is extensible to a multitude of activity. Britain has wasted many years, falling behind international comparison in all aspects of development of our living environment. Inherited infrastructure has decayed, provision for the future has been neglected. Not merely material quality of life has slipped, but also the less easily definable cultural environment and attributes. Public resources alone are never going to be available, nor enough, to fund all the development desirable. Partnership structures — in industry, education, physical and community development of all sorts — may possibly be the last chance to catch up before it is too late. We must not accept an 'equilibrium of stagnation' — an inability of government or institutions to deliver anything but an unsatisfactory re-hashing of what already inadequately exists.

Education the key

Education responds to the call of the prevailing culture. When it responds well its power is immense. If fully connected to a vision of an economic future that is ambitious, is shorn of complacency and seized of the danger of failing to compete internationally, it would be instrumental in revitalising our prospects. An enlivened understanding is needed of education's role in support of the economy, most especially in development of vocational and technical education. Economic and educational concern has to be driven forward in one combined attack.

The view that applied studies should be of equal value and status with the theoretical is far too little understood in this country, almost alone in the world. Does it never occur to us that our lone position in this respect, over long years, may be the common factor in the long story of our economic decline?

The academic skewing of our education, going back to the Victorian public school/university ethic of Arnold and Newman, has had the effect of skewing our attention and then consuming it. A devastating result is a system for the post-16s that for a *soi-disant* modern technological society is grossly inadequate — if not near ludicrous by international comparison.

The system needs to be complemented by parallel courses of technical and vocational education, of demanding character, leading to respected national qualifications. The absence of such provision has the real result, among others, of a huge deficiency of qualified engineers, designers, technologists and technicians, with extremely damaging consequences for Britain manufacturing and production — and so for the country's economic prosperity. A further result of 'the neglected middle' in post-16 provision has been foreseen. As modern, high-tech society moves on (at whatever pace), it may come to rest in another equilibrium, of skills, where the qualified population is evenly balanced by an underclass of servitors: and missing is the layer of middling qualified people who would otherwise release the elite to produce innovative movement. Escape from this bind lies in involvement of whole communities in expanding post-16 experience of quality — a huge development ground for partnership.

Lastly, again does it not occur to us that niggardly education provision over years has contributed to a level of national vulgarity, taste, social behaviour virtually unacceptable in the modern world? Our people deserve better than to have been treated like this, and the general quality of our society will not rapidly improve unless they are. There is a malign circle of cultural-social deprivation — underlying the economic problem, part it and deepening it — to be broken.

A last look forward

The prospect of Britain becoming irretrievably stuck in a slough without forward movement is not attractive, for us now or as trustees for our children and successors. The North of England has the capacity to pull itself out of such a mire, and surely wants the chance to exert its muscle to do so. Other regions of the kingdom, if they see themselves in similar plight, may take heart from a Northern intention and expression of spirit.

Hence St William's Foundation is glad to spread the news of its initiative, its 'Assertion of the North'. The initiative's success will depend absolutely on the effectiveness of the web of partnerships that can be woven; the Foundation will be equally glad to draw advantage from the experience of others creating their own versions of partnership. And, initiative succeeding, brighter futures for 15 million people in the North of England could light up a new way to many more.

References

1 Harrison, Michael, Assertion of the North, St William's Foundation, *Strategy Review* Part 1, January 1991.
2 Handy, Charles, 'What is a Company For?', Michael Shanks Memorial Lecture, *Royal Society of Arts Journal*, March 1991.

Chapter 11: Towards total quality in education

Bill Walton

The task of education business partnerships is to create, improve, protect and champion good learning environments; if they don't do this, they are an expensive waste of time and resources. Environments are created by their physical surroundings and the people in them. They are influenced by the beliefs which people have, which affect the ways in which they behave and in which they use their resources. Good learning in a democracy is underpinned by a belief in equal consideration and respect — that is everyone's entitlement; these are also the values of partnership. Learning encompasses understandings and skills, and their applications; learning informs our behaviour and attitudes — what we do and why. In our schools, learning...

> promotes the spiritual, moral, cultural, mental and physical development of pupils at the school and of society; and prepares such pupils for the opportunities, responsibilities and experiences of adult life. (*Section 1*. Education Reform Act 1988)[1].

Good learning environments are more than the sum of their parts; they are exciting, attractive, motivating and challenging for those within them. Partners have to reach a common understanding of good learning environments and of the conditions which produce them in order that they may jointly promote them. Unfortunately consensus isn't always in evidence amongst those who would claim to be in 'partnership'. It can happen that the business side assumes a dominant role in the diagnosis of educational problems and the formulation of solutions and that education is less than whole hearted in its co-operation with business. The emergence over the last few years of education as a matter of national priority has occurred largely in response to our economic situation and our performance in the international market place. This case is well put in the following quotation from a report to the United States Senate:

> the rate of change in society has increased dramatically during the last two centuries. Remarkable innovations in manufacturing, science, health care, technology, transportation and communications have resulted not only in new tools, products and services but also in new kinds of employment, demanding new skills with a reduced need for a large, low-skilled, industrial workforce. Education has created these capacities for change and must respond to these changes. There is a growing recognition by educators and others that traditional schooling does not adequately serve an increasingly large number of students. For the first time, schools must ensure the educational success of *all* students.[2]

It is unlikely that any report in the UK would be so brutally honest, but it accurately describes our situation, except that the inadequate nature of our provision for many students has long been recognised by many educators, and only becomes impor tant to others through economic necessity. The fact is that as a consequence of climbing out of the depression in the early 1980s, of remodelling our business processes, and of becoming a serious entrant into the high tech race, the work force profile has changed and will continue to change. At the same time the downturn in the number of young people entering the employment market has emphasised the need for a greater proportion of young people with the skills which successful businesses will require. Interestingly, the projected shortfall in the availability of skilled labour has done more for equal opportunity employment than more than a decade of educational programmes. Educational developments often occur in the wake of economic necessity. All this is well known and understood, but can pose problems for partnerships. Economic survival and the profit line are of critical importance to us all but successful partnerships must look beyond them. Material wealth is a means and not an end in itself — partners are interested in the quality of life for all, as well as the means of securing it.

Consensus has to be a necessary condition of partnership. It is difficult to achieve at the best of times, but is, perhaps, especially problematic in education. There is not, and probably never has been, agreement in this country on the aims, objectives, content and processes of education. Any successful business person will know that the lack of common vision, sense of direction and purpose provide a tested recipe for failure. Education is a huge business; there can be no doubt that educational achievement in the country suffers for the want of a common vision for it. The present position is especially unsatisfactory; instability and uncertainty follow the imposition of a major government programme for education without adequate consultation and in the face of substantial calls for modification. The process of working towards partnership through a common vision for education will require considerable commitment but offer great gains in understanding and ownership.

The recent legislation has changed considerably the balance of power and responsibility for public education. The power of local education authorities has been reduced whilst additional power has been given to central government and the revised and highly decentralised governing bodies of schools and colleges. The influence of the trade unions has been weakened as a consequence of legislation, our economic circumstances, and demographic decline. The net result is the concentration of effective power in the hands of the government. It is important in a democracy that there should be a balance of power in education to secure its impartiality and protect it from party political abuse. Partnerships, politically non-aligned bodies, have the opportunity to begin to re-establish a proper sense of balance. There is an urgent need for a powerful voice to speak for education when government policies and programmes are unrealistic, ill timed or inadequately resourced. For more than a decade there has been an inverse relationship between government policy on public expenditure and that on education; it has been low on funding and high on educational aspiration and expectation. There is a growing, often unstated, anticipation that the private sector will pick up the bill for public services. Partnerships should challenge the trend; partnerships should not be about alternative sources of funding for the public education service but about ensuring proper levels of public funding with additional support from the private sector. Partnerships will do well not to accede to requests for financial support for the bread and butter resources of schools.

Following on from the 1988 Education Act, government has introduced a very ambitious programme for education through its National Curriculum and testing schemes. There is much concern in schools and local education authorities for the speed of implementation of the programme, about the need to protect the educational entitlement of all young people during the period of implementation and for the level of resources being made available during the period of change. Partnerships will need to become knowledgeable about this situation and if they come to share the anxiety of many working in the field they should voice their concern. It will be the best schools and the most highly committed and able teachers who will suffer the greatest stress and hardship if they are constrained and over-burdened by insensitive administrations.

Local management of schools, the opportunities to opt out of the local education authority system, and funding formulae dominated by per capita allocations come together to provide a force for the fragmentation of the education service rather than the more desirable decentralisation. Partnerships should look at the case for an education service, in terms of the opportunities it presents for sensible planning, provision for population migration and demographic change, best use of scarce and expensive resources, effective curriculum and professional development, smooth transition between the ages and stages of education, and quality education for all those with special educational needs. If partnerships find the case proven they should consider how the tensions towards fragmentation might be reduced and how they might come to be a better understanding of the responsibilities and common commitments which are essential in any decentralised organisation.

The principles which underpin good work force relationships in business apply equally well in the education business. Business understands that continual criticism and complaint are not conducive to high motivation, high productivity and high quality. This is especially so if the criticism is directed against people who are working very hard, doing their best in, often, very difficult circumstances. Recent times have seen a catalogue of complaints against the teaching profession; standards of spelling, arithmetic and reading have come under attack from the government and in the media. Some of the claims have been on the basis of debatable information, and all have been highly selective and have only drawn attention to the adverse elements of research whilst ignoring much encouraging, positive information. A headline in the early weeks of 1991 referred to a 20% failure rate in reading skills; an alternative, and preferable, line would have been an 80% success rate and a reminder of the conclusion of the Warnock Committee that, at any one time, 18% of the school population has special educational needs. It is important to celebrate success in education; there is no shortage of good things happening in our schools and the teaching profession deserves more recognition for them. Partnerships will provide a valuable service if they emphasise success and draw attention to it.

The examination system has long been a serious bone of contention in this country. Successive governments have had their reform policies but many of the misgivings remain. The area of assessment of experience and performance is especially pertinent to partnerships. Partnerships have a strong vested interest in the quality of output of the examination system and in its cost-effectiveness. The examination business is big business with a multi-million pound turnover and with the possibility that it will grow in size, complexity and cost. Many of the costs are hidden in the time of teachers who are distracted from their primary task by the managerial and administrative requirements of examinations. Yet there is significant concern for the quality and reliability of the output of this examination system. The business world often expresses unhappiness about inadequate information on personal qualities and the poor correlation between examination performance and characteristics like enterprise, initiative, imagination, diligence, reliability and sense of personal and collective responsibility. Business no longer understands the examination system and its grades and it bemoans the continually changing scene; GCE adding CSE, becoming GCSE adding key stage 4, etc. It is seen as an esoteric process designed to confuse many of its legitimate users.

The will to comprehend the system would be greater if there was more confidence in the results of examinations. Many teachers recognise that examinations do not measure experience and achievement; they reflect the ability of the individual to respond to a number of questions, drawn from a substantial syllabus, at a particular time. They do not even reflect the cognitive side of learning; they are about the ability to recall and express accurately in a pressurised situation. They cannot respond to the totality of the experience and achievement of the individual. Often they are capable of manipulation by the enterprising student who will see question spotting as a less tedious alternative to committing the syllabus to memory. Examination results are doubtful predictors of capability; some research shows no positive correlation between first degree results and 'A' level results. Too often school examinations are concerned more with remembering than with understanding and applying knowledge. Partnership provides a forum for the consideration of the evidence and the opportunity to reach a view on it.

The extended partnership of business, local education service, university and polytechnic, in Sheffield has taken ownership of the Sheffield Record of Experience and Achievement. It is intended that the record will provide a profile of the experience and achievement of a young person at school. The creation, validation and accreditation of the record requires that the partnership understands it and takes ownership of it. It could be that a record of achievement which has been validated by the business community will carry greater credibility with business people inside and outside Sheffield than an examination award from one of the national examination boards.

The record of achievement has attractive spin-offs. It allows business people and those in higher education to demonstrate an interest and a commitment to the work of young people in schools. It provides a valid purpose for visiting schools on a regular basis which, coincidentally, allows business and higher education to better understand the workings of schools. Much of the conflict between education and business stems from mutual ignorance and misunderstanding.

The formative advantages of the record are considerable; it provides an on-going record which can be used for evaluative purposes by student, teacher and parent, and thereby a basis for the consideration of future planning of learning and teaching. The process of creating the record is valuable in its own right; it brings respect for the contribution of the parent to the learning environment and can provide a level of involvement by the parent which has rarely been seen in our schools.

Partnerships might consider the relative advantages and disadvantages of examination and record of achievement systems in terms of their cost-effectiveness, their reliability and breadth of application, their influence upon the curriculum, and on the teaching and learning time they consume.

Schools are businesses — a secondary school with 1,000 students may employ 65 staff and handle a revenue budget of about £1.8 million; it is a medium sized business. Schools are being required to take on more and more of the full range of business functions. In those areas, where in the interests of equity and efficiency, local management being extended to all schools, the small primary school will have the same range of managerial and administrative responsibilities as the large secondary school. The delegation of responsibility for local management is being introduced alongside National Curriculum and testing. At the same time schools continue to be responsible for the provision of high quality education for their students. In many cases the resources available to the schools during the period of change are being reduced. For some schools, especially primary schools, it will be the new managerial responsibilities which will bring the most daunting challenge. Many headteachers are unfamiliar with, and apprehensive about, the mysteries of financial, human resource and estate management, and aware that the local authorities, as a consequence of overall financial stringency and funding formulae for education, will only be able to provide limited support. The business side of partnership is well placed to significantly relieve the physical and psychological burden upon many schools. Financial management and the complexities of human resource and contract management are the bread and butter skills of many modern businesses. Individual contacts with schools, educator-into-business schemes, industrial secondments, and seminars all provide routes for the development of new skills and techniques and the provision of support and encouragement. A telephone number could provide access to a much appreciated help-line in some cases.

Reference has been made already to the debilitating effect of prolonged public criticism upon the morale of teachers and the potential damage it can have for educational standards. Unfortunately, there are other counter-productive forces at work which should be confronted.

The Secretary of State announced recently his intention to accelerate the introduction of an appraisal scheme for teachers. The business world is familiar with appraisal and would see developmental evaluation as an integral part of the process of good management. Unfortunately some of the rhetoric of this recent announcement has not been so enlightened, but has been couched in hard, aggressive language. It promises to 'sort out' poor teachers. Threatened people do not perform well — their energies tend to be diverted from the primary task. Business is familiar with the counter-productive nature of narrowly conceived appraisal; educators in schools need help in convincing their employers and the government of the importance of taking a developmental approach to appraisal. Undoubtedly the absence of a well thought out scheme of appraisal, including a major element of self-appraisal, followed by professional development programmes, has been a weakness in the personnel policies for education and should be remedied — business has the knowledge and experience to provide valuable assistance in this task.

Recent years have seen an increasing emphasis on the importance of inspection as a means of securing quality performance. The monitoring role of the LEA is clearly spelt out in the new legislation. DES has offered specific funding for the appointment of inspectors and some LEAs now have distinct advisory and inspectorial services. DES has not responded sympathetically to those LEAs which have maintained that they should have the opportunity to determine the most appropriate way of fulfilling their monitorial responsibility. Inspection has been a traditional feature of business. At best it has been an unwelcome overhead; often it has been a non-productive one. Regretfully traditional inspection often shifts the focus of responsibility for the quality of performance away from the person carrying out the work. Evidence of the cost effectiveness of inspections is hard to come by and on this basis alone it is an area of challenge for partnerships. Taken together with the other forces already mentioned in this chapter, increased levels of inspection become a potentially counter-productive measure. The clear message behind this and so much more of national policy at present is that teachers cannot be trusted. Teachers are told that what they do is vitally important, that they alone can translate and extend the National Curriculum into rich comprehensive learning opportunities and at the same time that they cannot be trusted to do the job. Of course quality and assessment of performance are important, and the government is right to insist that often in the past education has given inadequate attention to evaluation. But this does not mean that the outmoded and discredited instruments of business evaluation should be wished upon education. Partnerships should carefully examine the practices being introduced into schools and if they come to share the critique of this paper, they should condemn them.

Many successful companies in the most advanced industrial countries would attribute much of their success to revised approaches to quality assurance. They have recognised the direct relationship between trust on the one hand and ownership, responsibility, productivity and quality on the other. Many companies which have empowered their employees have seen impressive gains in productivity and quality and improvements in industrial relations. A British company operating in Indiana, USA, is taking an increasing proportion of the motor car piston business in the US and Europe. It is successful because it produces a high quality product on time at a price the customer can afford. The secret of its success lies in the empowerment of its employees; all inspection is the responsibility of the employees themselves, as is responsibility for the manufacturing process. The decision to stop the line is with the employee, as is the decision to review the production process. Employees have been given the time and the skills to match their responsibilities. Total quality is a developing concept, but it is applicable to the education business just as much as it is to any other business. Not only does education require support from business partners in prevailing upon government and employers to take a more enlightened approach to quality and productivity, total quality provides an area for joint developmental work between education and business to their mutual advantage. The gains would come not only in quality assurance and morale, but also in a better understanding of each other. Too often business has been inward looking and has not been sufficiently rigorous in pursuing the question of who needs to know of changes in its practices and needs. Perhaps the attitude developed during a long period of established practice and little change. The present pace of change, which is unlikely to slow, requires that business should maintain a close dialogue with education if the latter is to serve it well. There should be a place on the agenda of partnerships for matters like the direction of business development and its consequences for commercial and manufacturing processes and their work force requirements. This information is essential not only for good careers education but also to assist schools in providing an accurate picture of the local economic and business situation for their students. Schools have been accused of neglecting economic and industrial understanding and its relationship with social standards; partnerships have the opportunity to improve the quality of this aspect of the curriculum.

Some mention has been made already of the salutary effect which business support can have on motivation in schools. A year or so ago Business in the Community arranged for a number of the chief executives of some of the UK's largest national and international corporations to spend a day in a school. Their presence and interest alone did a lot for the morale of the schools involved. The schools particularly appreciated the supportive feedback, which was almost unanimous in its expressions of surprise for the complex nature and weight of responsibility of schools, of admiration for the skill and commitment of staff, and of concern for the level of resourcing. Obviously the leaders of major organisations cannot spend much of their time in schools, but their occasional visits would complement the very valuable support which can be given on a regular and consistent basis by businesses and people who work within them.

The USA has some impressive 'mentor' programmes whereby individuals from a business or the local community develop a close relationship with a student or group of youngsters. The programme has been particularly helpful where the mentor has been able to support the work of the school with pupils at risk and/or with special educational needs. The key feature of effective mentor schemes is a genuine consistent interest on the part of the mentor for the young person. The selection of mentors is a matter which requires considerable care, but the American experience is that it is worthwhile; successful arrangements can bring substantial gains in motivation and happiness to both partners.

Extending from the individual partnerships there are wide varieties of helpful relationships between groups or classes of children and a department of a business or a small company going on to whole business/school schemes. The aim of this arrangement is the same as that of the mentor programmes; it is to demonstrate in a consistent way that someone cares about, is interested in and encourages the school and its students in their work. Many schools and students do receive strong support from parents and local communities, but many, often those who need it most, do not. Just for a child to know that someone will be interested in her work or to have the opportunity to do something for someone else and know it will be appreciated can significantly change the child's attitude to the task. It sometimes happens that a business is well disposed to the idea of partnership but it feels it has little to offer; just to offer time may be very helpful and can bring dividends for both the partners.

Work-shadowing, whereby a student follows a business person during her normal work routines over a period of a few weeks is becoming increasingly commonplace in the UK. Provided that the shadow is adequately prepared and the shadowed person is willing to give sufficient time to introductions and explanations, it can be a productive experience. It can provide a young person with a good understanding of what work is like and what a particular career can offer as well as bringing confidence and enhancing their personal aspirations. For the shadowed person the time taken for explanation may bring an awareness that some of their routines may be ready for review.

All the various schemes of individual and school support allow business to demonstrate its support for education and prevocational training, and its commitment to the local community. In time this may bring improved relationships between company and the community and between employer and employees.

Contact between school and business leads naturally to, arguably, the most fruitful area for partnership — curriculum enhancement. Traditionally in our secondary schools there has been an overemphasis on content. Information has been put before young people in tight subject departments: maths, history, physics etc — with little attention paid to the relationships between the subjects and the applicability of their content to the outside world. It is hardly surprising that such a large percentage of young people 'fail' in a situation where school work holds little intrinsic value for them or their parents. Too often 'waste of time, better off getting a job' are the shared feelings of the young person and the parent. Success in education has come largely through a process of social indoctrination; if the young person has been brought up in a supportive home which was valued education and encouraged the youngster to stick at the work in order to pass through the hoops which lead to higher education and the professional occupations, the young person has very

often done well at school. Educational practice in this country
has acknowledged the cognitive side of learning but has often
neglected the affective side. We all know that our success as
learners depends very much upon how we feel about the content, whether it is interesting or worthwhile, and about the way
in which the learning is approached — whether we will have to
sit and listen or take notes, or whether we will be able to become
directly involved in the process and dictate its pace. Business
offers a tremendous and largely untapped wealth of opportunities for curriculum enrichment — content and process — with
many valuable spin-offs for both business and education. In
Sheffield the steel industry provides numerous vehicles which
can enable teachers to achieve their curriculum objectives in the
various subject domains in ways which are meaningful and
interesting for teachers, students and parents — all need to be
exploited in the good learning environment. Parents working at
all levels in businesses can begin to establish empathy with the
school work of their children and contribute to it in the workplace, or the school or at home. The mutual understanding and
growth of confidence which may be engendered by co-operative
working can have valuable implications for family and home/
school relationships.

Teachers seconded or given time to investigate the curriculum
opportunities which business offers, inevitably at the same time
become more aware of the world they prepare young people for.
For many teachers a business secondment breaks their personal
career cycle of school, university to school. Work experience for
teachers will help them to plan work experience for students as
an integrated part of the curriculum rather than an add-on to
provide some relief for the teacher but of little advantage to the
student and an inconvenience for business. Good, well thought
out industrial or commercial experience for teachers provides the
opportunity to spot the exciting curriculum vehicles and identify
the challenging and enterprising educational opportunities.

Secondment of business people to education brings gains for
business and its understanding of educational settings and
allows business people to reflect on how their expertise and
resources might help education. The involvement of business
can improve the credibility of curriculum offerings. There can be
no doubt that much of the success of the Young Enterprise
Scheme comes from the involvement of business people in it. If
the scheme was organised and judged by teachers alone it would
not catch the interest of young people and schools in the way
that is has. Business people may contribute to the actual delivery
of education. Obviously this requires confidence on both sides

and careful preparation; inviting someone into class on a Friday afternoon to talk about engineering can be a disaster, but a timely introduction of an engineer to a project on water power can add to the reality and interest of the work. Thoughtful attention to the choice of business visitors to classrooms can helpfully reinforce the equal opportunity aspect of the curriculum by challenging the discriminatory stereotyping of many professions. Ideally partnerships should allow teachers and business people to work together on curriculum developments and to consider jointly what each might offer to curriculum delivery. The narrowness of the academic content of many 'A' level courses has been a constant cause of complaint and concern over several years. The support of business could bring about a review of 16–19 education with the intention of integration of the pre-vocational and applied together with the academic curriculum. One of the fond hopes for the tertiary colleges established in Sheffield in 1988, by the bringing together of sixth form education and the further education colleges, was that the new 16–19 provision would draw upon the strengths of the partners. It was felt that combining the academic aspects of the sixth forms with the opportunities for applied study and more flexible course structures of further education could result in exciting new approaches to 16–19 education. Not only would the academic study be placed in relevant contexts but the students would come to have a much better understanding and expectation of higher education courses and what lies beyond them. The applied orientation of 16–19 work might make it more attractive to more students. It could also place some pressure upon the institutions of higher education to review both their admission arrangements and the context of their courses. One task of the engineer is to find high quality solutions to physical problems which take account of their social and economic implications. The traditional 'A' level route (maths, further maths and physics) into engineering does little to attract many of the most able, imaginative and enterprising young minds towards the profession.

As well as providing a worthwhile focus for study, business can enliven the process of education by offering hands-on opportunities, team work, enterprise and leadership situations. Some of the best partnership schemes are those where business offers support and resources to schools which are willing to tackle real problems. Business has been pleasantly surprised on many occasions by the quality of school work. Young people have shown considerable ingenuity, resourcefulness and determination in solving difficult industrial problems. For example, the managing director of an engineering company in Sheffield offered an aircraft kit to a school willing to take on the construction task. The assembly instructions were all written to US specification which provided an interesting conversion problem for the youngsters who took up the challenge. The building of the aircraft — this was the real thing not a toy — and the fabrication of many working parts to fine tolerances brought the students face to face with many new situations. They had to extend their knowledge of the behaviour of soft metals, learn to interpret complicated machine drawings, gain new machine shop skills, and accept the discipline of working as part of a team. They travelled backwards and forwards between school and industry, came to understand the work of a mechanical engineer and the processes of modern industrial engineering. The range and depth of learning and the sense of satisfaction and achievement gained by the students were of a level which could not have been reached in the classroom. Projects of this type generate high levels of motivation not only because they are worthwhile but also because they imply a high degree of confidence in the young people. They facilitate an understanding of the world of work and of the relationship between economic wealth and the quality of life. They bring respectability to industry in the eyes of young people and allow them to see that work can be rewarding, interesting and challenging.

These approaches should not be seen as peripheral to the school curriculum but as an integral part of it. The quality and breadth of learning can be of a very high order and entirely relevant to the needs of young people in modern society. The integrated approach to learning in a business or community context may begin to challenge some of the notions of curriculum content assumed to be unproblematic. Maybe partners will come to feel that schools will respond better to the aims of education set out in the 1988 Education Act if they are not tied to curricula based on the traditional subjects alone. Partners might feel that personal and social development should be set out clearly among the objectives of educational programmes. If partnerships do begin to question the established pillars of the secondary school curriculum they will certainly need to face the constraint placed on curriculum development by the National Curriculum and examination systems which dictate subject content. A 16 year old who spoke at a Young Enterprise presentation admitted that he was not much of a public speaker and that he had become disaffected with school where he had 'failed' regularly. He also spoke of the motivation and enjoyment he had derived from Young Enterprise and the confidence he had gained from this knowledge that he did possess significant, relevant abilities — school just had not teased them out before.

This paper set out to explore what education might gain from partnerships. The fact is that the interests of both education and industry are inseparable. Quality in one will not be sustained without quality in the other. The search for quality is the task of partnerships, and the criteria for quality partnerships are well known. They coincide with those which underpin successful businesses, classrooms and families. Real collegiality is based on trust and confidence — it can be relied upon to protect those it considers important. Such partnerships will provide strong, tangible support but will have high expectations. They will be enterprising and working continually to extend their knowledge base. They will be open and honest, but will be caring and will recognise and celebrate success. The decisions will be made at the appropriate level by those who have a stake in them. The UK is only beginning to realise the potential of partnerships; education has been shy to join hands with business and vice versa, but it has to happen. The Report by the Council of Chief State School Officers of the US [2] referred to the economic imperative of quality education for all, it is more than that — all young people have the right to quality education.

Education business partnerships, if they have the confidence, can create a broad balanced, integrated student-orientated curriculum which will embrace the hearts and minds of all young people.

References

1   DES, Education Reform Act, 1988, London, HMSO.
2   Report by the Council of Chief State School Officers of the US on restructuring education — 'Success for All in a New Century', November 1989.

Endpiece: Emerging themes and issues

Elizabeth Clough, Bob Gibbs and Roy Hedge

In this short piece we draw together the main themes which recur through the various contributions and which seem to us important.

The question of purpose is critical. The economic argument for partnerships is made powerfully in the book, in a way which emphasises that this is not just about producing a better skilled work force to create more capital. It is also about opportunity — for communities and individuals — to learn and to continue to learn, a learning that will have economic as well as other human benefit. That the worlds of business and education should learn from one another ought to be a truism, given that both worlds and cultures impinge on and shape most people's lives. It affects every citizen in the UK, in direct or indirect ways that, for example, the manufacturing sector of the economy has drastically shrunk or that large proportions of young people still leave full-time education and go on to experience only low-level, underfunded training thereafter. Nevertheless, in the UK at least, the value of education and business working together in partnership still needs assertion and justification. The purposes for specific partnership activities needs be both explicit and agreed, they need to benefit all partners and they need to transcend limited commercial purposes.

Education business partnerships, though recent in their current form, have antecedents which it would be foolish to ignore. There is always a danger of this happening with innovation, of those instigating and leading a new initiative coming to believe that nothing happened in the field before their arrival. Many people have worked hard over the last two decades to develop relationships between education and business — the expertise which this represents needs to be respected and harnessed. Otherwise, there is a real risk of innovation producing nothing that is substantially changed.

Different contributors to the volume have chosen to categorise partnerships in various ways. Partnerships differ in scope, purpose and specific orientation and in the nature of relationship they aspire to. Thus, partnerships can be conceived on a large scale — national projects or organisations such as the education business units within TECs, designed to serve large communities. On the other hand, they may be more modest in scope, represented, for example, by a school or college and the business community in its immediate locality. Partnerships differ, as well, in terms of specific purpose and therefore location on the whole partnership map. What is important here is that partnership activities have clear, explicit agreed aims which can be realistically achieved given the human and other resources allocated to them. What is also important, of course, and this we have barely begun to tackle, is that disparate partnership ventures learn of one another's existence, learn from one another and have some sense of their specific contribution to the wider vision. Thirdly, and this is the most challenging categorisation, partnerships differ in terms of the intimacy of education business relationships which are developed. To create partnerships which are incremental to understanding in both worlds, requires genuine collaboration in a trusting, learning climate, honest evaluation of experimentation and innovation and clarity about the power relationship between participating individuals and the organisations they represent. Commitment by organisations to partnership must come from the top, from managing directors and headteachers for example. It can only be realised fully by involving able people and delegating power and responsibility to them in ways which allow the whole organisation to take responsibility for outcomes and for future action. Many partnerships, of course, are characterised by much more superficial, less close relationships between education and business where, crucially, activities remain largely separate from the mainstream activities of both and owned only by those individuals who are involved rather their organisations.

Partnerships, small scale as well as large, need a clear sense of purpose made explicit in objectives, they need a strategic plan for achieving these objectives which is communicated to and understood by those involved and they need a review and evaluation process built into the whole to determine what is being achieved. Planning advice for those responsible for establishing partnerships of various kinds is now widely available. Rational planning models have several shortcomings — there is the danger that the plan becomes all important, the wider goals get lost. There is the danger that the plan becomes fossilised, static and unresponsive to new intelligence or other changed circumstances. The most serious danger, however, is that the 'people bit' gets lost — plans often assume that people will work and prosecute them in logical, rational ways, which of course they do not. The reality is a good deal messier and more risky for those managing the change. The temptation is always to deny this rather than confront it, to revert to plans on paper, stick with the safe rather than the exciting even if, at the end of the day with this route, little is achieved.

In order to continue to learn about the practical potentials of partnership we must devise intelligent ways of gathering information about quality developments. Such evaluation must carry realistic expectations about the timescales and pace of change which is possible in partnership activities. Given the complex interpersonal relationships and the cultural differences between education and business, partnerships must allow time for people to change and for things to happen. Partnerships need guidance and support to help those involved to continually reflect on previous learning and to plan change on the basis of this reflection. This represents an evaluation style which can at least begins to examine quality from a human stand point — it is a far cry from kite marks and British Standards. The importance of review and evaluation as an integral part of the strategic management of partnerships cannot be overemphasised. It is the area that is most often relegated to the 'we'll do that when there's time' list and, when it is undertaken, it is in forms that are threatening, unrealistic, irrelevant, time consuming and unused. The rapidity of change and development in and around partnerships demands that review and evaluation is embedded into the day to day action at all levels of the organisation. This will require training and development in review and evaluation approaches, skills and techniques for key members of the partnership.

Finally partnership activity will have to be funded adequately if it is to achieve much worthwhile. Such backing must come from national government — the issues are too big for the responsibility of generating finance to be handed down to more local levels. Partnership on the cheap, with for example only short term planning possible, and people on short term contracts will make little, if any, difference to the habitual ways in which education and business have traditionally related to one another.

Notes on contributors

MICHAEL AUSTIN has been Principal at Accrington and Rossendale College, one of the longest established tertiary colleges in the country, since 1981. He is President of the Tertiary Colleges Association, a founder member of the Further Education Campaign Group and an executive member of the Postsecondary International Network.

ELIZABETH CLOUGH has considerable research experience in the area of education, training and work. She has managed partnership projects linking the interests of major engineering companies with the education service and has published widely in the fields of personal and organisational learning. She is currently Senior Consultant with Partnership Consultancy and holds an Honorary Lectureship at the University of Sheffield.

PETER DAVIES was appointed Project Director of the Teacher Placement Service in April 1989 from his previous post as Southern Area Director of Understanding British Industry. His previous experience is based on a teaching career in Somerset, which included a long secondment to the University of Leicester.

GRAHAM ELLIOTT has taught in a range of schools and was the Adviser for Careers Education and Guidance in Sheffield for seven years prior to taking up his present post as the Headteacher of Hinde House School, Sheffield. His experience in careers education and working with parents is documented in a number of publications.

BILL FISHER is the Yorkshire and Humberside Regional Manager for the Teacher Placement Service, part of the Understanding British Industry initiative. He has taught in primary, secondary and higher education and his recent professional experience covers a variety of education business projects, including the School Curriculum Industry Partnership.

BOB GIBBS acquired production management experience in industry and then moved into education where he gained wide experience of staff training and organisational development. He has worked on several education business projects and authored several publications on educational and industrial change. At present he is Senior Consultant with Partnership Consultancy and is an Honorary Lecturer at the University of Sheffield.

HARRY GRAY is currently Higher Education Adviser to the Employment Department. He has lectured on many aspects of

180   The Reality of Partnership

educational management and authored books and articles on human aspects of management. For a time he was a management consultant specialising in education and small businesses.

MICHAEL HARRISON was Chief Education Officer for the City of Sheffield, was formerly a member of the Engineering Council and of the Yorkshire and Humberside Regional Economic Planning Council. He is a council member of St William's Foundation, York, chairing its Forward Strategy and Programme Working Group.

ROY HEDGE has wide experience in education and consultancy work in the UK and the USA. Currently, he is Senior Consultant with Partnership Consultancy. He has held senior management posts in education and local government including the Directorship of Sheffield's School Focused Development Programme from 1986–90. His experience in managing change and initiating innovative staff and organisational development approaches is documented in a number of publications.

JOHN KRACHAI has experience in both business and education. He was the Owner/Director of a successful design/manufacturing business before moving into school teaching and advisory work in LEAs. He was recently Director of Sheffield's Education Business Partnership and has contributed to the partnership debate both in the UK and the USA.

SEAN LAWLOR has wide school teaching experience, including the setting up of a school support unit in a London comprehensive. He was subsequently appointed as an Advisory Teacher for the Disruptive Pupils' Programme for the Inner London Education Authority. In 1981 he became School Curriculum Industry Partnership Co-ordinator in Tower Hamlets. Since 1990 he has worked as an independent educational consultant.

ANDREW MILLER is the Research and Development Director with the School Curriculum Industry Partnership/Mini-Enterprise in Schools Project, a major national link body committed to promoting partnerships between schools and industry. He is the author of many publications on aspects of the work-related curriculum and schools/industry links.

BILL WALTON was formerly Chief Education Officer for the City of Sheffield and a founder signatory of the Sheffield Education Business Partnership. He is a member of the Business in the Community Task Group on Education Business Partnerships and was a member of the council of the Federation of Education Business Partnerships.

JOHN WOOLHOUSE is Professor of Education at the University of Warwick and is Director of the Centre for Education and Industry there. After 18 years with Rolls-Royce, he became Assistant Director of Kingston Polytechnic in 1972. In 1978 he joined an international consulting firm, where he directed projects in the UK and in developing countries. From 1983–88 he was Director of TVEI.

IVAN YATES was, until 1990, Deputy Chief Executive (Engineering), British Aerospace. He currently serves as Vice President of AECMA (Association Europeenne des Constructeurs de Materiel Aerospatial) where he oversees technical activities within European aerospace trade associations. He is a former President of the Society of British Aerospace Companies; a council member of the Fellowship of Engineers; and a council member of the Royal Aeronautical Society.